Principle of Management

Dr.K. Lingadurai

Dr.K. Raja

Published by

ISBN 978-93-84743-35-2
Author

Dr.K. Lingadurai

Dr.K. Raja

Bonfring
309, 2nd Floor, 5th Street Extension, Gandhipuram,
Coimbatore-641 012.
Tamilnadu, India.
E-mail: info@bonfring.org
Website: www.bonfring.org
Phone: 0422-3928700

<table>
<tr><th>Unit</th><th>Contents</th><th>Page No</th></tr>
</table>

Unit I

Overview of Management

1.1.   Definition

According to Harold Koontz, "Management is an art of getting things done through and with the people in formally organized groups. It is an art of creating an environment in which people can perform and individuals and can co-operate towards attainment of group goals".

1.2.   Levels of Management

The three levels of management are as following Fig 1.1.

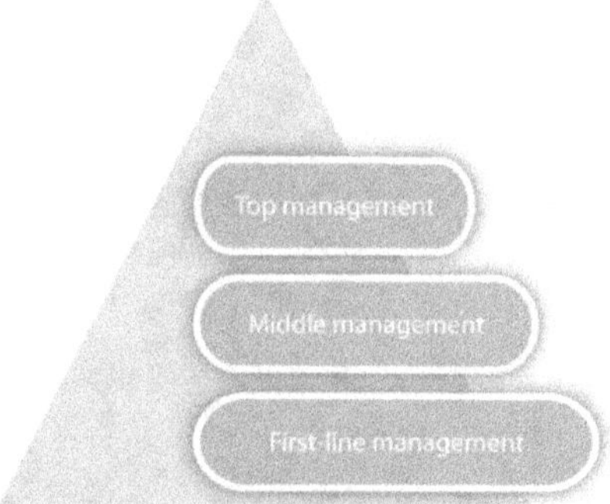

Fig 1.1: Levels of Management

1.2.1.   The Top Level Management

It consists of board of directors, chief executive or managing director. The top management is the ultimate source of authority and it manages goals and policies for an enterprise. It devotes more time on planning and coordinating functions. The role of the top management can be summarized as follows :

- Top management lays down the objectives and broad policies of the enterprise.
- It issues necessary instructions for preparation of department budgets, procedures, schedules etc.
- It prepares strategic plans & policies for the enterprise.
- It appoints the executive for middle level i.e. departmental managers.
- It controls & coordinates the activities of all the departments.

- It is also responsible for maintaining a contact with the outside world.
- It provides guidance and direction.
- The top management is also responsible towards the shareholders for the performance of the enterprise.

1.2.2. *Middle Level Management*

The branch managers and departmental managers constitute middle level. They are responsible to the top management for the functioning of their department. They devote more time to organizational and directional functions. In small organization, there is only one layer of middle level of management but in big enterprises, there may be senior and junior middle level management. Their role can be emphasized as -

- They execute the plans of the organization in accordance with the policies and directives of the top management.
- They make plans for the sub-units of the organization.
- They participate in employment & training of lower level management.
- They interpret and explain policies from top level management to lower level.
- They are responsible for coordinating the activities within the division or department.
- It also sends important reports and other important data to top level management.
- They evaluate performance of junior managers.
- They are also responsible for inspiring lower level managers towards better performance.

1.2.3. *Lower Level Management*

It is also known as supervisory/operative level of management. It consists of supervisors, foreman,section officers, superintendent etc. According to R.C. Davis, "Supervisory management refers to those executives whose work has to be largely with personal oversight and direction of operative employees". In other words, they are concerned with direction and controlling function of management. Their activities include

- Assigning of jobs and tasks to various workers.
- They guide and instruct workers for day to day activities.
- They are responsible for the quality as well as quantity of production.
- They are also entrusted with the responsibility of maintaining good relation in the organization.

- They communicate workers problems, suggestions, and recommendatory appeals etc to the higher level and higher level goals and objectives to the workers.
- They help to solve the grievances of the workers.
- They supervise & guide the sub-ordinates.
- They are responsible for providing training to the workers.

1.3.   Functions of Management

Management has been described as a social process involving responsibility for economical and effective planning & regulation of operation of an enterprise in the fulfillment of given purposes. It is a dynamic process consisting of various elements and activities. These activities are different from operative functions like marketing, finance, purchase etc. Rather these activities are common to each and every manger irrespective of his level or status. Different experts have classified functions of management. According to George & Jerry, "There are four fundamental functions of management i.e. planning, organizing, actuating and controlling". According to Henry Fayol, "To manage is to forecast and plan, to organize, to command, & to control". Whereas Luther Gullick has given a keyword 'POSDCORB' where P stands for Planning, 0 for Organizing, S for Staffing, D for Directing, Co for Co-ordination, R for reporting & B for Budgeting. But the most widely accepted are functions of management given by KOONTZ and O'DONNEL i.e. **Planning, Organizing, Staffing, Directing** and **Controlling.** For theoretical purposes, it may be convenient to separate the function of management but practically these functions are overlapping in nature i.e. they are highly inseparable. Each function blends into the other & each affects the performance of others. The Functions of Management is explained in the following Fig 1.2.

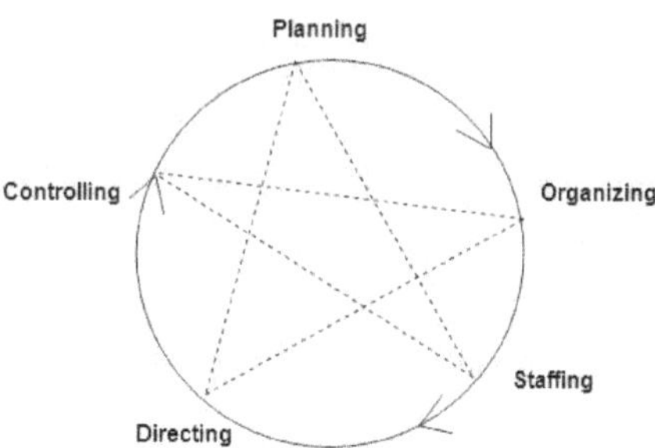

Fig 1.2: Functions of Management

1. *Planning*

It is the basic function of management. It deals with chalking out a future course of action & deciding in advance the most appropriate course of actions for achievement of pre-determined goals. According to KOONTZ, "Planning is deciding in advance - what to do, when to do & how to do. It bridges the gap from where we are & where we want to be". A plan is a future course of actions. It is an exercise in problem solving & decision making. Planning is determination of courses of action to achieve desired goals. Thus, planning is a systematic thinking about ways & means for accomplishment of predetermined goals. Planning is necessary to ensure proper utilization of human & non-human resources. It is all pervasive, it is an intellectual activity and it also helps in avoiding confusion, uncertainties, risks, wastages etc.

2. *Organizing*

It is the process of bringing together physical, financial and human resources and developing productive relationship amongst them for achievement of organizational goals. According to Henry Fayol, "To organize a business is to provide it with everything useful or its functioning i.e. raw material, tools, capital and personnel's". To organize a business involves determining & providing human and non-human resources to the organizational structure. Organizing as a process involves:

- Identification of activities.
- Classification of grouping of activities.
- Assignment of duties.
- Delegation of authority and creation of responsibility.
- Coordinating authority and responsibility relationships.

3. *Staffing*

It is the function of manning the organization structure and keeping it manned. Staffing has assumed greater importance in the recent years due to advancement of technology, increase in size of business, complexity of human behavior etc. The main purpose o staffing is to put right man on right job i.e. square pegs in square holes and round pegs in round holes. According to Kootz & O'Donell, "Managerial function of staffing involves manning the organization structure through proper and effective selection, appraisal & development of personnel to fill the roles designed un the structure".

Staffing involves:

- Manpower Planning (estimating man power in terms of searching, choose the person and giving the right place)
- Recruitment, selection & placement
- Training & development
- Remuneration
- Performance appraisal
- Promotions & transfer

4. Directing

It is that part of managerial function which actuates the organizational methods to work efficiently for achievement of organizational purposes. It is considered life-spark of the enterprise which sets it in motion the action of people because planning, organizing and staffing are the mere preparations for doing the work. Direction is that inert-personnel aspect of management which deals directly with influencing, guiding, supervising, motivating sub-ordinate for the achievement of organizational goals. Direction has following elements:

- Supervision
- Motivation
- Leadership
- Communication

i. **Supervision:** Implies overseeing the work of subordinates by their superiors. It is the act of watching & directing work & workers.

ii. **Motivation:** Means inspiring, stimulating or encouraging the sub-ordinates with zeal to work. Positive, negative, monetary, non-monetary incentives may be used for this purpose.

iii. **Leadership:** May be defined as a process by which manager guides and influences the work of subordinates in desired direction.

iv. **Communications:** Is the process of passing information, experience, opinion etc from one person to another. It is a bridge of understanding.

5. *Controlling*

It implies measurement of accomplishment against the standards and correction of deviation if any to ensure achievement of organizational goals. The purpose of controlling is to ensure that everything occurs in conformities with the standards. An efficient system of control helps to predict deviations before they actually occur. According to Theo Haimann, "Controlling is the process of checking whether or not proper progress is being made towards the objectives and goals and acting if necessary, to correct any deviation". According to Koontz & O'Donell "Controlling is the measurement & correction of performance activities of subordinates in order to make sure that the enterprise objectives and plans desired to obtain them as being accomplished".

Therefore controlling has following steps:

i. Establishment of standard performance.
ii. Measurement of actual performance.
iii. Comparison of actual performance with the standards and finding out deviation if any.
iv. Corrective action.

1.4. Roles of Manager

Henry Mintzberg identified ten different roles, separated into three categories. The categories he defined are as following Fig 1.3.

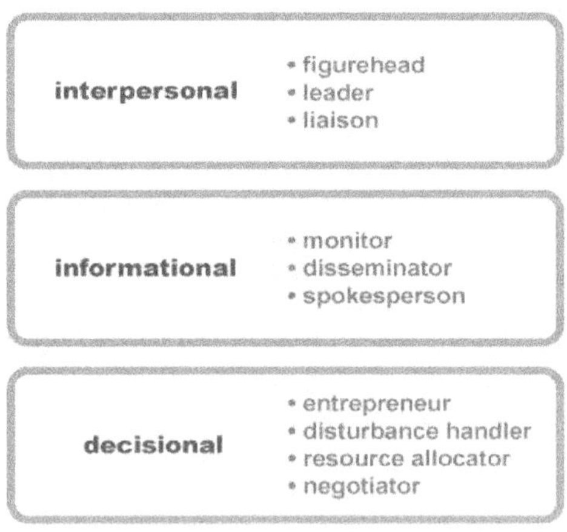

Fig 1.3: Roles of Manager

a) *Interpersonal Roles*

The ones that, like the name suggests, involve people and other ceremonial duties. It can be further classified as follows.

- Leader - Responsible for staffing, training, and associated duties.
- Figurehead - The symbolic head of the organization.
- Liaison - Maintains the communication between all contacts and informers that compose the organizational network.

b) *Informational Roles*

Related to collecting, receiving and disseminating information.

- Monitor-Personally seek and receive information, to be able to understand the organization.
- Disseminator-Transmits all import information received from outsiders to the members of the organization.
- Spokesperson-On the contrary to the above role, here the manager transmits the organization's plans, policies and actions to outsiders.

c) *Decisional Roles*

Roles that revolve around making choices.

- Entrepreneur-Seeks opportunities. Basically they search for change, respond to it, and exploit it.
- Negotiator-Represents the organization at major negotiations.
- Resource Allocator-Makes or approves all significant decisions related to the allocation of resources.
- Disturbance Handler-Responsible for corrective action when the organization faces disturbances.

1.5. Evolution of Management thought

The practice of management is as old as human civilization. The ancient civilizations of Egypt (the great pyramids), Greece (leadership and war tactics of Alexander the great) and Rome displayed the marvelous results of good management practices.

The origin of management as a discipline was developed in the late 19th century. Over time, management thinkers have sought ways to organize and classify the voluminous information about management that has been collected and disseminated. These attempts at classification have resulted in the identification of management approaches. The approaches of management are theoretical frameworks for the study of management. Each of the approaches of management is based on somewhat different assumptions about human beings and the organizations for which they work.

The different approaches of management are

(a) Classical approach

(b) Behavioral approach

(c) Quantitative approach

(d) Systems approach

(e) Contingency approach.

The formal study of management is largely a twentieth-century phenomenon, and to some degree the relatively large number of management approaches reflects a lack of consensus among management scholars about basic questions of theory and practice.

1.5.1. *The Classical Approach*

The classical approach is the oldest formal approach of management thought. Its roots pre-date the twentieth century. The classical approach of thought generally concerns ways to manage work and organizations more efficiently. Three areas of study that can be grouped under the classical approach are scientific management, administrative management, and bureaucratic management,

i. *Scientific Management*

Frederick Winslow Taylor is known as the father of scientific management. Scientific management (also called Taylorism or the Taylor system) is a theory of management that analyzes and synthesizes workflows, with the objective of improving labor productivity. In other words, Traditional rules of thumb are replaced by precise procedures developed after careful study of an individual at work.

ii. *Administrative Management*

Administrative management focuses on the management process and principles of management. In contrast to scientific management, which deals largely with jobs and work at the individual level of analysis, administrative management provides a more general theory of management. Henri Fayol is the major contributor to this approach of management thought.

iii. *Bureaucratic Management*

Bureaucratic management focuses on the ideal form of organization. Max Weber was the major contributor to bureaucratic management. Based on observation, Weber concluded that many early organizations were inefficiently managed, with decisions based on personal relationships and loyalty. He proposed that a form of organization, called a bureaucracy, characterized by division of labor, hierarchy, formalized rules, impersonality, and the selection and promotion of employees based on ability, would lead to more efficient management. Weber also contended that managers' authority in an organization should be based not on tradition or charisma but on the position held by managers in the organizational hierarchy.

1.5.2. *The Behavioral Approach*

The behavioral approach of management thought developed, in part, because of perceived weaknesses in the assumptions of the classical approach. The classical approach emphasized efficiency, process, and principles. Some felt that this emphasis disregarded important aspects of organizational life, particularly as it related to human behavior. Thus, the behavioral approach focused on trying to understand the factors that affect human behavior at work,

i. *Human Relations*

The Hawthorne Experiments began in 1924 and continued through the early 1930s. A variety of researchers participated in the studies, including Elton Mayo. One of the major conclusions of the Hawthorne studies was that workers' attitudes are associated with productivity. Another was that the workplace is a social system and informal group influence could exert a powerful effect on individual behavior. A third was that the style of supervision is an important factor in increasing workers' job satisfaction,

ii. *Behavioral Science*

Behavioral science and the study of organizational behavior emerged in the 1950s and 1960s. The behavioral science approach was a natural progression of the human relations movement. It focused on applying conceptual and analytical tools to the problem of understanding and predicting behavior in the workplace.

The behavioral science approach has contributed to the study of management through its focus on personality, attitudes, values, motivation, group behavior, leadership, communication, and conflict, among other issues.

1.5.3. The Quantitative Approach

The quantitative approach focuses on improving decision making via the application of quantitative techniques. Its roots can be traced back to scientific management,

i.   Management Science (Operations Research)

Management science (also called operations research) uses mathematical and statistical approaches to solve management problems. It developed during World War II as strategists tried to apply scientific knowledge and methods to the complex problems of war. Industry began to apply management science after the war. The advent of the computer made many management science tools and concepts more practical for industry.

ii.   Production and Operations Management

This approach focuses on the operation and control of the production process that transforms resources into finished goods and services. It has its roots in scientific management but became an identifiable area of management study after World War II. It uses many of the tools of management science.

Operations management emphasizes productivity and quality of both manufacturing and service organizations. W. Edwards Deming exerted a tremendous influence in shaping modern ideas about improving productivity and quality. Major areas of study within operations management include capacity planning, facilities location, facilities layout, materials requirement planning, scheduling, purchasing and inventory control, quality control, computer integrated manufacturing, just-in-time inventory systems, and flexible manufacturing systems.

1.5.4. Systems Approach

The systems approach focuses on understanding the organization as an open system that transforms inputs into outputs. The systems approach began to have a strong impact on management thought in the 1960s as a way of thinking about managing techniques that would allow managers to relate different specialties and parts of the company to one another, as well as to external environmental factors. The systems approach focuses on the organization as a whole, its interaction with the environment, and its need to achieve equilibrium.

1.5.5. *Contingency Approach*

The contingency approach focuses on applying management principles and processes as dictated by the unique characteristics of each situation. It emphasizes that there is no one best way to manage and that it depends on various situational factors, such as the external environment, technology, organizational characteristics, characteristics of the manager, and characteristics of the subordinates. Contingency theorists often implicitly or explicitly criticize the classical approach for its emphasis on the universality of management principles; however, most classical writers recognized the need to consider aspects of the situation when applying management principles.

MANAGEMENT APPROACHS	Beginning Dates	Emphasis
CLASSICAL APPROACH		
Scientific Management	1880s	Traditional rules of thumb are replaced by precise procedures developed after careful study of an individual at work.
Administrative Management	1940s	Gives idea about the primary functions of management and The 14 Principles of Administration
Bureaucratic Management	1920s	Replaces traditional leadership and charismatic leadership with legal leadership
BEHAVIORAL APPROACH		
Human Relations	1930s	workers' attitudes are associated with productivity
Behavioral Science	1950s	Gives idea to understand human behavior in the organization.
QUANTITATIVE APPROACH		
Management Science (Operation research)	1940s	Uses mathematical and statistical approaches to solve management problems.
Production and Operations Management	1940s	This approach focuses on the operation and control of the production process that transforms resources into finished goods and services
RECENT DEVELOPEMENTS		
Systems Approach	1950s	Considers the organization as a system that transforms inputs into outputs while in constant interaction with its' environment.
Contingency Approach	1960s	Applies management principles and processes as dictated by the unique characteristics of each situation.

1.6. Contribution of Fayol and Taylor

F.W.Taylor and Henry Fayol are generally regarded as the founders of scientific management and administrative management and both provided the bases for science and art of management.

1.6.1. *Taylor's Scientific Management*

Frederick Winslow Taylor well-known as the founder of scientific management was the first to recognize and emphasis the need for adopting a scientific approach to the task of managing an enterprise. He tried to diagnose the causes of low efficiency in industry and came to the conclusion that much of waste and inefficiency is due to the lack of order and system in the methods of management. He found that the management was usually ignorant of the amount of work that could be done by a worker in a day as also the best method of doing the job. As a result, it remained largely at the mercy of the workers who deliberately shirked work. He therefore, suggested that those responsible for management should adopt a scientific approach in their work, and make use of "scientific method" for achieving higher efficiency. The scientific method consists essentially of

(a) Observation

(b) Measurement

(c) Experimentation and

(d) Inference.

He advocated a thorough planning of the job by the management and emphasized the necessity of perfect understanding and co-operation between the management and the workers both for the enlargement of profits and the use of scientific investigation and knowledge in industrial work. He summed up his approach in these words:

- Science, not rule of thumb
- Harmony, not discord
- Co-operation, not individualism
- Maximum output, in place of restricted output
- The development of each man to his greatest efficiency and prosperity.

1.6.2. *Elements of Scientific Management*

The techniques which Taylor regarded as its essential elements or features may be classified as under:

1. Scientific Task and Rate-setting, work improvement, etc.
2. Planning the Task
3. Vocational Selection and Training
4. Standardization (of working conditions, material equipment etc.)
5. Specialization
6. Mental Revolution

1. Scientific Task and Rate-Setting (Work Study)

Work study may be defined as the systematic, objective and critical examination of all the factors governing the operational efficiency of any specified activity in order to effect improvement. Work study includes.

Methods Study: The management should try to ensure that the plant is laid out in the best manner and is equipped with the best tools and machinery. The possibilities of eliminating or combining certain operations may be studied.

Motion Study: It is a study of the movement, of an operator (or even of a machine) in performing an operation with the purpose of eliminating useless motions.

Time Study (work measurement): The basic purpose of time study is to determine the proper time for performing the operation. Such study may be conducted after the motion study. Both time study and motion study help in determining the best method of doing a job and the standard time allowed for it.

(a) **Fatigue Study:** If, a standard task is set without providing for measures to eliminate fatigue, it may either be beyond the workers or the workers may over strain themselves to attain it. It is necessary, therefore, to regulate the working hours and provide for rest pauses at scientifically determined intervals.

(b) **Rate-setting:** Taylor recommended the differential piece wage system, under which workers performing the standard task within prescribed time are paid a much higher rate per unit than inefficient workers who are not able to come up to the standard set.

2. Planning the Task

Having set the task which an average worker must strive to perform to get wages at the higher piece-rate, necessary steps have to be taken to plan the production thoroughly so that there is no bottlenecks and the work goes on systematically.

3. Selection and Training

Scientific Management requires a radical change in the methods and procedures of selecting workers. It is therefore necessary to entrust the task of selection to a central personnel department. The procedure of selection will also have to be systematized. Proper attention has also to be devoted to the training of the workers in the correct methods of work.

4. *Standardization*

Standardization may be introduced in respect of the following.

(a) **Tools and equipment:** By standardization is meant the process of bringing about uniformity. The management must select and store standard tools and implements which will be nearly the best or the best of their kind.

(b) **Speed:** There is usually an optimum speed for every machine. If it is exceeded, it is likely to result in damage to machinery.

(c) **Conditions of Work:** To attain standard performance, the maintenance of standard conditions of ventilation, heating, cooling, humidity, floor space, safety etc., is very essential.

(d) **Materials:** The efficiency of a worker depends on the quality of materials and the method of handling materials.

5. *Specialization*

Scientific management will not be complete without the introduction of specialization. Under this plan, the two functions of 'planning' and 'doing' are separated in the organization of the plant. The A functional foremen' are specialists who join their heads to give thought to the planning of the performance of operations in the workshop. Taylor suggested eight functional foremen under his scheme of functional foremanship.

(a) **The Route Clerk:** To lay down the sequence of operations and instruct the workers concerned about it.

(b) **The Instruction Card Clerk:** To prepare detailed instructions regarding different aspects of work.

(c) **The Time and Cost Clerk:** To send all information relating to their pay to the workers and to secure proper returns of work from them.

(d) **The Shop Disciplinarian:** To deal with cases of breach of discipline and absenteeism.

(e) **The Gang Boss:** To assemble and set up tools and machines and to teach the workers to make all their personal motions in the quickest and best way.

(f) **The Speed Boss:** To ensure that machines are run at their best speeds and proper tools are used by the workers.

(g) **The Repair Boss:** To ensure that each worker keeps his machine in good order and maintains cleanliness around him and his machines.

(h) **The Inspector:** To show to the worker how to do the work.

6. *Mental Revolution*

At present, industry is divided into two groups - management and labour. The major problem between these two groups is the division of surplus. The management wants the maximum possible share of the surplus as profit; the workers want, as large share in the form of wages. Taylor has in mind the enormous gain that arises from higher productivity. Such gains can be shared both by the management and workers in the form of increased profits and increased wages.

1.6.3. *Henry Fayol's 14 Principles of Management*

The principles of management are given below:

1. **Division of work:** Division of work or specialization alone can give maximum productivity and efficiency. Both technical and managerial activities can be performed in the best manner only through division of labour and specialization.

2. **Authority and Responsibility:** The right to give order is called authority. The obligation to accomplish is called responsibility. Authority and Responsibility are the two sides of the management coin. They exist together. They are complementary and mutually interdependent.

3. **Discipline:** The objectives, rules and regulations, the policies and procedures must be honored by each member of an organization. There must be clear and fair agreement on the rules and objectives, on the policies and procedures. There must be penalties (punishment) for non-obedience or indiscipline. No organization can work smoothly without discipline - preferably voluntary discipline.

4. **Unity of Command:** In order to avoid any possible confusion and conflict, each member of an organization must received orders and instructions only from one superior (boss).

5. **Unity of Direction:** All members of an organization must work together to accomplish common objectives.

6. **Emphasis on Subordination of Personal Interest to General or Common Interest:** This is also called principle of co-operation. Each shall work for all and all for each. General or common interest must be supreme in any joint enterprise.

7. **Remuneration:** Fair pay with non-financial rewards can act as the best incentive or motivator for good performance. Exploitation of employees in any manner must be eliminated. Sound scheme of remuneration includes adequate financial and non-financial incentives.

8. **Centralization:** There must be a good balance between centralization and decentralization of authority and power. Extreme centralization and decentralization must be avoided.

9. **Scalar Chain:** The unity of command brings about a chain or hierarchy of command linking all members of the organization from the top to the bottom. Scalar denotes steps.

10. **Order:** Fayol suggested that there is a place for everything. Order or system alone can create a sound organization and efficient management.

11. **Equity:** An organization consists of a group of people involved in joint effort. Hence, equity (i.e., justice) must be there. Without equity, we cannot have sustained and adequate joint collaboration.

12. **Stability of Tenure:** A person needs time to adjust himself with the new work and demonstrate efficiency in due course. Hence, employees and managers must have job security. Security of income and employment is a pre-requisite of sound organization and management.

13. **Esprit of Co-operation:** Esprit de corps is the foundation of a sound organization. Union is strength. But unity demands co-operation. Pride, loyalty and sense of belonging are responsible for good performance.

14. **Initiative:** Creative thinking and capacity to take initiative can give us sound managerial planning and execution of predetermined plans.

1.7. Organization and Environmental Factors

An organization is a group of people intentionally organized to accomplish a common or set of goals.

1.7.1. Types of Business Organizations

When organizing a new business, one of the most important decisions to be made is choosing the structure of a business.

a) Sole Proprietorships

The vast majority of small business starts out as sole proprietorships . . . very dangerous. These firms are owned by one person, usually the individual who has day-to-day responsibility for running the business. Sole proprietors own all the assets of the business and the profits generated by it. They also assume "complete personal" responsibility for all of its liabilities or debts. In the eyes of the law, you are one in the same with the business.

Merits

- Easiest and least expensive form of ownership to organize.
- Sole proprietors are in complete control, within the law, to make all decisions.
- Sole proprietors receive all income generated by the business to keep or reinvest.
- Profits from the business flow-through directly to the owner's personal tax return.
- The business is easy to dissolve, if desired.

Demerits

- Unlimited liability and are legally responsible for all debts against the business.
- Their business and personal assets are 100% at risk.
- Has almost been ability to raise investment funds.
- Are limited to using funds from personal savings or consumer loans.
- Have a hard time attracting high-caliber employees, or those that are motivated by the opportunity to own a part of the business.
- Employee benefits such as owner's medical insurance premiums are not directly deductible from business income (partially deductible as an adjustment to income).

b) Partnerships

In a Partnership, two or more people share ownership of a single business. Like proprietorships, the law does not distinguish between the business and its owners. The Partners should have a legal agreement that sets forth how decisions will be made, profits will be shared, disputes will be resolved, how future partners will be admitted to the partnership, how partners can be bought out, or what steps will be taken to dissolve the partnership when needed. Yes, its hard to think about a "break-up" when the business is just getting started, but many partnerships split up at crisis times and unless there is a defined process, there will be even greater problems. They also must decide up front how much time and capital each will contribute, etc.

Merits

- Partnerships are relatively easy to establish; however time should be invested in developing the partnership agreement.
- With more than one owner, the ability to raise funds may be increased.
- The profits from the business flow directly through to the partners' personal taxes.
- Prospective employees may be attracted to the business if given the incentive to become a partner.

Demerits

- Partners are jointly and individually liable for the actions of the other partners.
- Profits must be shared with others.
- Since decisions are shared, disagreements can occur.
- Some employee benefits are not deductible from business income on tax returns.
- The partnerships have a limited life; it may end upon a partner withdrawal or death.

c) *Corporations*

A corporation, chartered by the state in which it is headquartered, is considered by law to be a unique "entity", separate and apart from those who own it. A corporation can be taxed; it can be sued; it can enter into contractual agreements. The owners of a corporation are its share holders.The shareholders elect a board of directors to oversee the major policies and decisions. The corporation has a life of its own and does not dissolve when ownership changes.

Merits

- Shareholders have limited liability for the corporation's debts or judgments against the corporations.
- Generally, shareholders can only be held accountable for their investment in stock of the company. (Note however, that officers can be held personally liable for their actions, such as the failure to withhold and pay employment taxes.)
- Corporations can raise additional funds through the sale of stock.
- A corporation may deduct the cost of benefits it provides to officers and employees.
- Can elect S corporation status if certain requirements are met. This election enables company to be taxed similar to a partnership.

Demerits

- The process of incorporation requires more time and money than other forms of organization.
- Corporations are monitored by federal, state and some local agencies, and as a result may have more paperwork to comply with regulations.
- Incorporating may result in higher overall taxes. Dividends paid to shareholders are not deductible form business income, thus this income can be taxed twice.

d) *Joint Stock Company*

Limited financial resources & heavy burden of risk involved in both of the previous forms of organization has led to the formation of joint stock companies these have limited dilutives. The capital is raised by selling shares of different values. Persons who purchase the shares are called shareholder. The managing body known as; Board of Directors; is responsible for policy making important financial & technical decisions. There are two main types of joint stock Companies.

i.   Private limited company

ii.   Public limited company

(i) *Private Limited Company*

This type company can be formed by two or more persons. Te maximum number of member ship is limited to 50. In this transfer of shares is limited to members only. The government also does not interfere in the working of the company,

(ii) *Public Limited Company*

Its is one whose membership is open to general public. The minimum number required to form such company is seven, but there is no upper limit. Such company's can advertise to offer its share to genera public through a prospectus. These public limited companies are subjected to greater control & supervision of control.

Merits

- The liability being limited the shareholder bear no Rick& therefore more as make persons are encouraged to invest capital.
- Because of large numbers of investors, the risk of loss is divided.
- Joint stock companies are not affected by the death or the retirement of the shareholders.

Demerits

- It is difficult to preserve secrecy in these companies.
- It requires a large number of legal formalities to be observed.
- Lack of personal interest.

e) Public Corporations

A public corporation is wholly owned by the Government centre to state. It is established usually by a Special Act of the parliament. Special statute also prescribes its management pattern power duties & jurisdictions. Though the total capital is provided by the Government, they have separate entity & enjoy independence in matters related to appointments, promotions etc.

Merits

- These are expected to provide better working conditions to the employees & supported to be better managed.
- Quick decisions can be possible, because of absence of bureaucratic control.
- More Flexibility as compared to departmental organization.
- Since the management is in the hands of experienced & capable directors & managers, these ate managed more efficiently than that of government departments.

Demerits

- Any alteration in the power & Constitution of Corporation requires an amendment in the particular Act, which is difficult & time consuming.
- Public Corporations possess monopoly & in the absence of competition, these are not interested in adopting new techniques & in making improvement in their working.

f) Government Companies

A state enterprise can also be organized in the form of a Joint stock company; A government company is any company in which of the share capital is held by the central government or partly by central government & party by one to more state governments. It is managed b the elected board of directors which may include private individuals. These are accountable for its working to the concerned ministry or department & its annual report is required to be placed ever year on the table of the parliament or state legislatures along with the comments of the government to concerned department.

Merits

- It is easy to form.
- The directors of a government company are free to take decisions & are not bound by certain rigid rules & regulations.

Demerits

- Misuse of excessive freedom cannot be ruled out.
- The directors are appointed by the government so they spend more time in pleasing their political masters & top government officials, which results in inefficient management.

1.7.2. Classification of Environmental Factors

On the basis of the extent of intimacy with the firm, the environmental factors may be classified into different types namely internal and external. The classification of Environmental factors is explained in the following Fig 1.4.

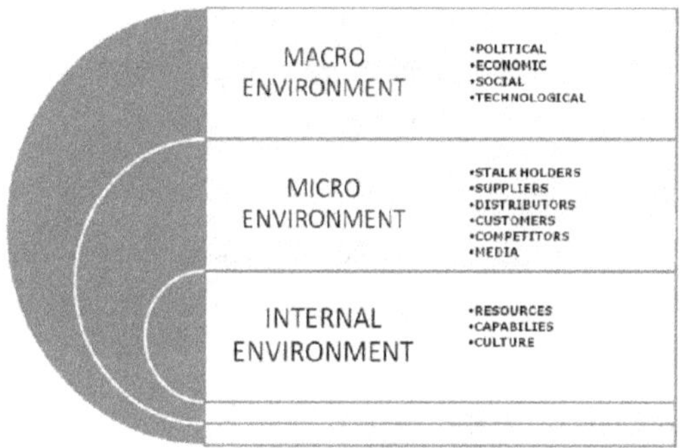

Fig 1.4: Environmental Factors

Internal Environmental Factors

The internal environment is the environment that has a direct impact on the business. The internal factors are generally controllable because the company has control over these factors.

It can alter or modify these factors. The internal environmental factors are resources, capabilities and culture.

i. Resources

A good starting point to identify company resources is to look at tangible, intangible and human resources. Tangible resources are the easiest to identify and evaluate: financial resources and physical assets are identifies and valued in the firm's financial statements. Intangible resources are largely invisible, but over time become more important to the firm than tangible assets because they can be a main source for a competitive advantage. Such intangible recourses include reputational assets (brands, image, etc.) and technological assets (proprietary technology and know-how). Human resources or human capital are the productive services human beings offer the firm in terms of their skills, knowledge, reasoning, and decision-making abilities.

ii.   Capabilities

Resources are not productive on their own. The most productive tasks require that resources collaborate closely together within teams. The term organizational capabilities are used to refer to a firm's capacity for undertaking a particular productive activity. Our interest is not in capabilities per se, but in capabilities relative to other firms. To identify the firm's capabilities we will use the functional classification approach. A functional classification identifies organizational capabilities in relation to each of the principal functional areas.

iii.   Culture

It is the specific collection of values and norms that are shared by people and groups in an organization and that helps in achieving the organizational goals.

External Environment Factors

It refers to the environment that has an indirect influence on the business. The factors are uncontrollable by the business. The two types of external environment are micro environment and macro environment.

a) Micro Environmental Factors

These are external factors close to the company that have a direct impact on the organizations process. These factors include:

i.   Shareholders

Any person or company that owns at least one share (a percentage of ownership) in a company is known as shareholder. A shareholder may also be referred to as a "stockholder". As organization requires greater inward investment for growth they face increasing pressure to move from private ownership to public. However this movement unleashes the forces of shareholder pressure on the strategy of organizations.

ii.   Suppliers

An individual or an organization involved in the process of making a product or service available for use or consumption by a consumer or business user is known as supplier. Increase in raw material prices will have a knock on affect on the marketing mix strategy of an organization. Prices may be forced up as a result. A closer supplier relationship is one way of ensuring competitive and quality products for an organization.

iii.   *Distributors*

Entity that buys non-competing products or product-lines, warehouses them, and resells them to retailers or direct to the end users or customers is known as distributor. Most distributors provide strong manpower and cash support to the supplier or manufacturer's promotional efforts.They usually also provide a range of services (such as product information, estimates, technical support, after-sales services, credit) to their customers. Often getting products to the end customers can be a major issue for firms. The distributors used will determine the final price of the product and how it is presented to the end customer. When selling via retailers, for example, the retailer has control over where the products are displayed, how they are priced and how much they are promoted in-store. You can also gain a competitive advantage by using changing distribution channels.

iv.   *Customers*

A person, company, or other entity which buys goods and services produced by another person, company, or other entity is known as customer. Organizations survive on the basis of meeting the needs, wants and providing benefits for their customers. Failure to do so will result in a failed business strategy.

v.   *Competitors*

A company in the same industry or a similar industry which offers a similar product or service is known as competitor. The presence of one or more competitors can reduce the prices of goods and services as the companies attempt to gain a larger market share. Competition also requires companies to become more efficient in order to reduce costs. Fast-food restaurants McDonald's and Burger King are competitors, as are Coca-Cola and Pepsi, and Wal-Mart and Target.

vi.   *Media*

Positive or adverse media attention on an organizations product or service can in some cases make or break an organization.. Consumer programmer with a wider and more direct audience can also have a very powerful and positive impact, forcing organizations to change their tactics.

b) *Macro Environmental Factors*

An organization's macro environment consists of nonspecific aspects in the organization's surroundings that have the potential to affect the organization's strategies. When compared to a firm's task environment, the impact of macro environmental variables is less direct and the organization has a more limited impact on these elements of the environment. The macro environment consists of forces that originate outside of an organization and generally cannot be altered by actions of the organization. In other words, a firm may be influenced by changes within this element of its environment, but cannot itself influence the environment. The curved lines in Figure 1 indicate the indirect influence of the environment on the organization.

Macro environment includes political, economic, social and technological factors. A firm considers these as part of its environmental scanning to better understand the threats and opportunities created by the variables and how strategic plans need to be adjusted so the firm can obtain and retain competitive advantage.

i.   *Political Factors*

Political factors include government regulations and legal issues and define both formal and informal rules under which the firm must operate. Some examples include:

- tax policy
- employment laws
- environmental regulations
- trade restrictions and tariffs
- political stability

ii.   *Economic Factors*

Economic factors affect the purchasing power of potential customers and the firm's cost of capital. The following are examples of factors in the macro economy:

- economic growth
- interest rates
- exchange rates
- inflation rate

iii.   *Social Factors*

Social factors include the demographic and cultural aspects of the external macro environment. These factors affect customer needs and the size of potential markets. Some social factors include:

- health consciousness
- population growth rate
- age distribution

- career attitudes
- emphasis on safety

iv.   *Technological Factors*

Technological factors can lower barriers to entry, reduce minimum efficient production levels, and influence outsourcing decisions. Some technological factors include:

- R&D activity
- automation
- technology incentives
- rate of technological change

1.8.   Trends and Challenges of Management in Global Scenario

The management functions are planning and decision making, organizing, leading, and controlling-are just as relevant to international managers as to domestic managers. International managers need to have a clear view of where they want their firm to be in the future; they have to organize to implement their plans: they have to motivate those who work lot them; and they have to develop appropriate control mechanisms.

a) Planning and Decision Making in a Global Scenario

To effectively plan and make decisions in a global economy, managers must have a broad-based understanding of both environmental issues and competitive issues. They need to understand local market conditions and technological factor that will affect their operations. At the corporate level, executives need a great deal of information to function effectively. Which markets are growing? Which markets are shrinking? Which are our domestic and foreign competitors doing in each market? They must also make a variety of strategic decisions about their organizations. For example, if a firm wishes to enter market in France, should it buy a local firm there, build a plant, or seek a strategic alliance? Critical issues include understanding environmental circumstances, the role of goals and planning in a global organization, and how decision making affects the global organization.

b) Organizing in a Global Scenario

Managers in international businesses must also attend to a variety of organizing issues. For example, General Electric has operations scattered around the globe. The firm has made the decision to give local managers a great deal of responsibility for how they run their business. In contrast, many Japanese firms give managers of their foreign operations relatively little responsibility. As a result, those managers must frequently travel back to Japan to present problems or get decisions approved. Managers in an international business must address the basic issues of organization structure and design, managing change, and dealing with human resources.

c) *Leading in a Global Scenario*

We noted earlier some of the cultural factors that affect international organizations. Individual managers must be prepared to deal with these and other factors as they interact people from different cultural backgrounds .Supervising a group of five managers, each of whom is from a different state in the United States, is likely to be much simpler than supervising a group of five managers, each of whom is from a different culture. Managers must understand how cultural factors affect individuals. How motivational processes vary across cultures, how the role of leadership changes in different cultures, how communication varies across cultures, and how interpersonal and group processes depend on cultural background.

d) *Controlling in a Global Scenario*

Finally, managers in international organizations must also be concerned with control. Distances, time zone differences, and cultural factors also play a role in control. For example, in some cultures, close supervision is seen as being appropriate, whereas in other cultures, it is not Like wise, executives in the United States and Japan may find it difficult to communicate vital information to one another because of the time zone differences. Basic control issues for the international manager revolve around operations management productivity, quality, technology and information systems.

UNIT II

PLANNING

2.1. Definition

According to Koontz O'Donnell - "Planning is an intellectual process, the conscious determination of courses of action, the basing of decisions on purpose, acts and considered estimates".

2.2. Nature and Purpose of Planning

Nature of Planning

- **Planning is goal-oriented:** Every plan must contribute in some positive way towards the accomplishment of group objectives. Planning has no meaning without being related to goals.

- **Primacy of Planning:** Planning is the first of the managerial functions. It precedes all other management functions.

- **Pervasiveness of Planning:** Planning is found at all levels of management. Top management looks after strategic planning. Middle management is in charge of administrative

  planning. Lower management has to concentrate on operational planning.

- **Efficiency, Economy and Accuracy:** Efficiency of plan is measured by its contribution to the objectives as economically as possible. Planning also focuses on accurate forecasts.

- **Co-ordination:** Planning co-ordinates the what, who, how, where and why of planning. Without co-ordination of all activities, we cannot have united efforts.

- **Limiting Factors:** A planner must recognize the limiting factors (money, manpower etc) and formulate plans in the light of these critical factors.

- **Flexibility:** The process of planning should be adaptable to changing environmental conditions.

- **Planning is an intellectual process:** The quality of planning will vary according to the quality of the mind of the manager.

Purpose of Planning

As a managerial function planning is important due to the following reasons:-

- **To manage by objectives:** All the activities of an organization are designed to achieve certain specified objectives. However, planning makes the objectives more concrete by focusing attention on them.
- **To offset uncertainty and change:** Future is always full of uncertainties and changes. Planning foresees the future and makes the necessary provisions for it.
- **To secure economy in operation:** Planning involves, the selection of most profitable course of action that would lead to the best result at the minimum costs.
- **To help in co-ordination:** Co-ordination is, indeed, the essence of management, the planning is the base of it. Without planning it is not possible to co-ordinate the different activities of an organization.
- **To make control effective:** The controlling function of management relates to the comparison of the planned performance with the actual performance. In the absence of plans, a management will have no standards for controlling other's performance.
- **To increase organizational effectiveness:** Mere efficiency in the organization is not important; it should also lead to productivity and effectiveness. Planning enables the manager to measure the organizational effectiveness in the context of the stated objectives and take further actions in this direction.

Features of Planning

- It is primary function of management.
- It is an intellectual process.
- Focuses on determining the objectives.
- Involves choice and decision making.
- It is a continuous process.
- It is a pervasive function.

2.3. Classification of Planning

On the Basis of Content

Strategic Planning

- It is the process of deciding on Long-term objectives of the organization.
- It encompasses all the functional areas of business.

Tactical Planning

- It involves conversion of detailed and specific plans into detailed and specific action plans.
- It is the blue print for current action and it supports the strategic plans.

On the Basis of Time Period

Long Term Planning

- Time frame beyond five years.
- It specifies what the organization wants to become in long run.
- It involves great deal of uncertainty.

Intermediate Term Planning

- Time frame between two and five years.
- It is designed to implement long term plans.

Short Term Planning

- Time frame of one year or less.
- It provide basis for day to day operations.

2.4. Planning Process

The various steps involved in planning are given below Fig 2.1.

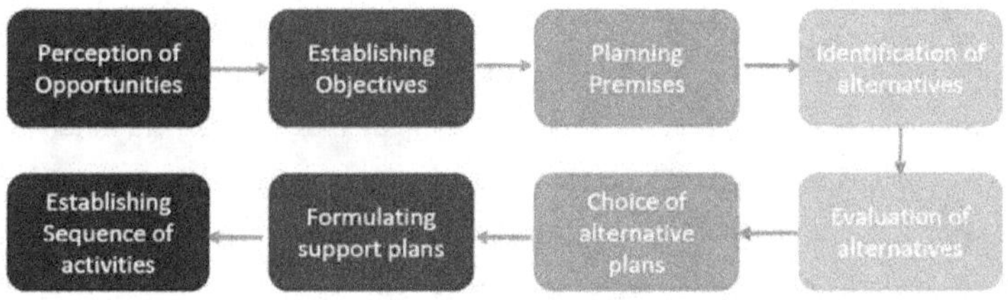

Fig 2.1: Planning Process

a) *Perception of Opportunities*

Although preceding actual planning and therefore not strictly a part of the planning process, awareness of an opportunity is the real starting point for planning. It includes a preliminary look at possible future opportunities and the ability to see them clearly and completely, knowledge of where we stand in the light of our strengths and weaknesses, an understanding of why we wish to solve uncertainties, and a vision of what we expect to gain. Setting realistic objectives depends on this awareness. Planning requires realistic diagnosis of the opportunity situation.

b) *Establishing Objectives*

The first step in planning itself is to establish objectives for the entire enterprise and then for each subordinate unit. Objectives specifying the results expected indicate the end points of what is to be done, where the primary emphasis is to be placed, and what is to be accomplished by the network of strategies, policies, procedures, rules, budgets and programs.

Enterprise objectives should give direction to the nature of all major plans which, by reflecting these objectives, define the objectives of major departments. Major department objectives, in turn, control the objectives of subordinate departments, and so on down the line. The objectives of lesser departments will be better framed, however, if subdivision managers understand the overall enterprise objectives and the implied derivative goals and if they are given an opportunity to contribute their ideas to them and to the setting of their own goals.

c) *Planning Premises*

Another logical step in planning is to establish, obtain agreement to utilize and disseminate critical planning premises. These are forecast data of a factual nature, applicable basic policies, and existing company plans. Premises, then, are planning assumptions - in other words, the expected environment of plans in operation. This step leads to one of the major principles of planning. The more individuals charged with planning understand and agree to utilize consistent planning premises, the more coordinated enterprise planning will be. Planning premises include far more than the usual basic forecasts of population, prices, costs, production, markets, and similar matters. Because the future environment of plans is so complex, it would not be profitable or realistic to make assumptions about every detail of the future environment of a plan.

Since agreement to utilize a given set of premises is important to coordinate planning, it becomes a major responsibility of managers, starting with those at the top, to make sure that subordinate managers understand the premises upon which they are expected to plan. It is not unusual for chief executives in well- managed companies to force top managers with differing views, through group deliberation, to arrive at a set of major premises that all can accept.

d) *Identification of Alternatives*

Once the organizational objectives have been clearly stated and the planning premises have been developed, the manager should list as many available alternatives as possible for reaching those objectives.

The focus of this step is to search for and examine alternative courses of action, especially those not immediately apparent. There is seldom a plan for which reasonable alternatives do not exist, and quite often an alternative that is not obvious proves to be the best. The more common problem is not finding alternatives, but reducing the number of alternatives so that the most promising may be analyzed. Even with mathematical techniques and the computer, there is a limit to the number of alternatives that may be examined. It is therefore usually necessary for the planner to reduce by preliminary examination the number of alternatives to those promising the most fruitful possibilities or by mathematically eliminating, through the process of approximation, the least promising ones.

e) *Evaluation of Alternatives*

Having sought out alternative courses and examined their strong and weak points, the following step is to evaluate them by weighing the various factors in the light of premises and goals. One course may appear to be the most profitable but require a large cash outlay and a slow payback; another may be less profitable but involve less risk; still another may better suit the company in long-range objectives.

If the only objective were to examine profits in a certain business immediately, if the future were not uncertain, if cash position and capital availability were not worrisome, and if most factors could be reduced to definite data, this evaluation should be relatively easy. But typical planning is replete with uncertainties, problems of capital shortages, and intangible factors, and so evaluation is usually very difficult, even with relatively simple problems. A company may wish to enter a new product line primarily for purposes of prestige; the forecast of expected results may show a clear financial loss, but the question is still open as to whether the loss is worth the gain.

f) *Choice of Alternative Plans*

An evaluation of alternatives must include an evaluation of the premises on which the alternatives are based. A manager usually finds that some premises are unreasonable and can therefore be excluded from further consideration. This elimination process helps the manager determine which alternative would best accomplish organizational objectives.

g) *Formulating of Supporting Plans*

After decisions are made and plans are set, the final step to give them meaning is to numberize them by converting them to budgets. The overall budgets of an enterprise represent the sum total of income and expenses with resultant profit or surplus and budgets of major balance-sheet items such as cash and capital expenditures. Each department or program of a business or other enterprise can have its own budgets, usually of expenses and capital expenditures, which tie into the overall budget. If this process is done well, budgets become a means of adding together the various plans and also important standards against which planning progress can be measured.

h) *Establishing Sequence of Activities*

Once plans that furnish the organization with both long-range and short-range direction have been developed, they must be implemented. Obviously, the organization can not directly benefit from planning process until this step is performed.

2.5. Types of Plans/Components of Planning

In the process of planning, several plans are prepared which are known as components of planning.

Plans can be broadly classified as,

a) Strategic plans

b) Tactical plans

c) Operational plans

Operational plans lead to the achievement of tactical plans, which in turn lead to the attainment of strategic plans. In addition to these three types of plans, managers should also develop a contingency plan in case their original plans fail.

a) *Strategic Plans*

A strategic plan is an outline of steps designed with the goals of the entire organization as a whole in mind, rather than with the goals of specific divisions or departments. It is further classified as

i. *Mission*

The mission is a statement that reflects the basic purpose and focus of the organization which normally remain unchanged. The mission of the company is the answer of the question : why does the organization exists?

Properly crafted mission statements serve as filters to separate what is important from what is not, clearly state which markets will be served and how, and communicate a sense of intended direction to the entire organization.

Mission of Ford: "we are a global, diverse family with a proud inheritance, providing exceptional products and services"

ii. *Objectives or Goals*

Both goal and objective can be defined as statements that reflect the end towards which the organization is aiming to achieve. However, there are significant differences between the two. A goal is an abstract and general umbrella statement, under which specific objectives can be clustered. Objectives are statements that describe—in precise, measurable, and obtainable terms which reflect the desired organization's outcomes.

iii. *Strategies*

Strategy is the determination of the basic long term objectives of an organization and the adoption of action and collection of action and allocation of resources necessary to achieve these goals. Strategic planning begins with an organization's mission. Strategic plans look ahead over the next two, three, five, or even more years to move the organization from where it currently is to where it wants to be. Requiring multilevel involvement, these plans demand harmony among all levels of management within the organization. Top-level management develops the directional objectives for the entire organization, while lower levels of management develop compatible objectives and plans to achieve them. Top management's strategic plan for the entire organization becomes the framework and sets dimensions for the lower level planning.

b) *Tactical Plans*

A tactical plan is concerned with what the lower level units within each division must do, how they must do it, and who is in charge at each level. Tactics are the means needed to activate a strategy and make it work.

Tactical plans are concerned with shorter time frames and narrower scopes than are strategic plans. These plans usually span one year or less because they are considered short-term goals. Long-term goals, on the other hand, can take several years or more to accomplish. Normally, it is the middle manager's responsibility to take the broad strategic plan and identify specific tactical actions.

c) *Operational Plans*

The specific results expected from departments, work groups, and individuals are the operational goals. These goals are precise and measurable. "Process 150 sales applications each week" or "Publish 20 books this quarter" are examples of operational goals. An operational plan is one that a manager uses to accomplish his or her job responsibilities. Supervisors, team leaders, and facilitators develop operational plans to support tactical plans (see the next section). Operational plans can be a single-use plan or a standing plan.

i. **Single-use plans** apply to activities that do not recur or repeat. A one-time occurrence, such as a special sales program, is a single-use plan because it deals with the who, what, where, how, and how much of an activity.

    Programme: Programme consists of an ordered list of events to be followed to execute a project.

    Budget: A budget predicts sources and amounts of income and how much they are used for a specific project.

ii. **Standing plans** are usually made once and retain their value over a period of years while undergoing periodic revisions and updates. The following are examples of ongoing plans:

    Policy: A policy provides a broad guideline for managers to follow when dealing with important areas of decision making. Policies are general statements that explain how a manager should attempt to handle routine management responsibilities. Typical human resources policies, for example, address such matters as employee hiring, terminations, performance appraisals, pay increases, and discipline.

Procedure: A procedure is a set of step-by-step directions that explains how activities or tasks are to be carried out. Most organizations have procedures for purchasing supplies and equipment, for example. This procedure usually begins with a supervisor completing a purchasing requisition. The requisition is then sent to the next level of management for approval. The approved requisition is forwarded to the purchasing department. Depending on the amount of the request, the purchasing department may place an order, or they may need to secure quotations and/or bids for several vendors before placing the order. By defining the steps to be taken and the order in which they are to be done, procedures provide a standardized way of responding to a repetitive problem.

Rule: A rule is an explicit statement that tells an employee what he or she can and cannot do. Rules are "do" and "don't" statements put into place to promote the safety of employees and the uniform treatment and behavior of employees. For example, rules about tardiness and absenteeism permit supervisors to make discipline decisions rapidly and with a high degree of fairness.

d) Contingency Plans

Intelligent and successful management depends upon a constant pursuit of adaptation, flexibility, and mastery of changing conditions. Strong management requires a "keeping all options open" approach at all times-that's where contingency planning comes in. Contingency planning involves identifying alternative courses of action that can be implemented if and when the original plan proves inadequate because of changing circumstances. Keep in mind that events beyond a manager's control may cause even the most carefully prepared alternative future scenarios to go awry. Unexpected problems and events frequently occur. When they do, managers may need to change their plans. Anticipating change during the planning process is best in case things don't go as expected. Management can then develop alternatives to the existing plan and ready them for use when and if circumstances make these alternatives appropriate.

2.6.   Objectives

Objectives may be defined as the goals which an organization tries to achieve. Objectives are described as the end- points of planning. According to Koontz and O'Donnell, "an objective is a term commonly used to indicate the end point of a management programmed." Objectives constitute the purpose of the enterprise and without them no intelligent planning can take place.

Objectives are, therefore, the ends towards which the activities of the enterprise are aimed. They are present not only the end-point of planning but also the end towards which organizing, directing and controlling are aimed. Objectives provide direction to various activities. They also serve as the benchmark of measuring the efficiency and effectiveness of the enterprise.

Objectives make every human activity purposeful. Planning has no meaning if it is not related to certain objectives.

2.6.1. Features of Objectives

- The objectives must be predetermined.
- A clearly defined objective provides the clear direction for managerial effort.
- Objectives must be realistic.
- Objectives must be measurable.
- Objectives must have social sanction.
- All objectives are interconnected and mutually supportive.
- Objectives may be short-range, medium-range and long-range.
- Objectives may be constructed into a hierarchy.

Advantages of Objectives

- Clear definition of objectives encourages unified planning.
- Objectives provide motivation to people in the organization.
- When the work is goal-oriented, unproductive tasks can be avoided.
- Objectives provide standards which aid in the control of human efforts in an organization.
- Objectives serve to identify the organization and to link it to the groups upon which its existence depends.
- Objectives act as a sound basis for developing administrative controls.
- Objectives contribute to the management process: they influence the purpose of the organization, policies, personnel, leadership as well as managerial control.

2.6.2. Process of Setting Objectives

Objectives are the keystone of management planning. It is the most important task of management. Objectives are required to be set in every area which directly and vitally effects the survival and prosperity of the business. In the setting of objectives, the following points should be borne in mind.

- Objectives are required to be set by management in every area which directly and vitally affects the survival and prosperity of the business.

- The objectives to be set in various areas have to be identified.

- While setting the objectives, the past performance must be reviewed, since past performance indicates what the organization will be able to accomplish in future.

- The objectives should be set in realistic terms i.e., the objectives to be set should be reasonable and capable of attainment.

- Objectives must be consistent with one and other.

- Objectives must be set in clear-cut terms.

- For the successful accomplishment of the objectives, there should be effective communication.

2.7. Management by Objectives (MBO)

MBO was first popularized by Peter Drucker in 1954 in his book 'The practice of Management'. It is a process of agreeing within an organization so that management and employees buy into the objectives and understand what they are. It has a precise and written description objectives ahead, timelines for their motoring and achievement. The employees and manager agree to what the employee will attempt to achieve in a period ahead and the employee will accept and buy into the objectives.

Definition

"MBO is a process whereby the superior and the mangers of an organization jointly identify its common goals, define each individual's major area of responsibility in terms of results expected of him, and use these measures as guides for operating the unit and assessing the contribution of each of its members."

2.7.1. Features of MBO

- MBO is concerned with goal setting and planning for individual managers and their units.

- The essence of MBO is a process of joint goal setting between a supervisor and a subordinate.

- Managers work with their subordinates to establish the performance goals that are consistent with their higher organizational objectives.

- MBO focuses attention on appropriate goals and plans.

- MBO facilitates control through the periodic development and subsequent evaluation of individual goals and plans.

2.7.2. Steps in MBO

The typical MBO process consists of

1) Establishing a clear and precisely defined statement of objectives for the employee
2) Developing an action plan indicating how these objectives are to be achieved
3) Reviewing the performance of the employees
4) Appraising performance based on objective achievement

1. Setting Objectives

For Management by Objectives (MBO) to be effective, individual managers must understand the specific objectives of their job and how those objectives fit in with the overall company objectives set by the board of directors. The managers of the various units or sub-units, or sections of an organization should know not only the objectives of their unit but should also actively participate in setting these objectives and make responsibility for them. Management by Objective (MBO) systems, objectives are written down for each level of the organization, and individuals are given specific aims and targets. Managers need to identify and set objectives both for themselves, their units, and their organizations.

2. Developing Action Plans

Actions plans specify the actions needed to address each of the top organizational issues and to reach each of the associated goals, who will complete each action and according to what timeline. An overall, top-level action plan that depicts how each strategic goal will be reached is developed by the top level management. The format of the action plan depends on the objective of the organization.

3. Reviewing Progress

Performance is measured in terms of results. Job performance is the net effect of an employee's effort as modified by abilities, role perceptions and results produced. Effort refers to the amount of energy an employee uses in performing a job. Abilities are personal characteristics used in performing a job and usually do not fluctuate widely over short periods of time. Role perception refers to the direction in which employees believe they should channel their efforts on their jobs, and they are defined by the activities and behaviors they believe are necessary.

4. *Performance Appraisal*

Performance appraisals communicate to employees how they are performing their jobs, and they establish a plan for improvement. Performance appraisals are extremely important to both employee and employer, as they are often used to provide predictive information related to possible promotion. Appraisals can also provide input for determining both individual and organizational training and development needs. Performance appraisals encourage performance improvement. Feedback on behavior, attitude, skill or knowledge clarifies for employees the job expectations their managers hold for them. In order to be effective, performance appraisals must be supported by documentation and management commitment.

Advantages

- Motivation - Involving employees in the whole process of goal setting and increasing employee empowerment. This increases employee job satisfaction and commitment.
- Better communication and Coordination-Frequent reviews and interactions between superiors and subordinates helps to maintain harmonious relationships within the organization and also to solve many problems.
- Clarity of goals
- Subordinates have a higher commitment to objectives they set themselves than those imposed on them by another person.
- Managers can ensure that objectives of the subordinates are linked to the organization's objectives.

Limitations

There are several limitations to the assumptive base underlying the impact of managing by objectives, including:

- It over-emphasizes the setting of goals over the working of a plan as a driver of outcomes.
- It underemphasizes the importance of the environment or context in which the goals are set. That context includes everything from the availability and quality of resources, to relative buy-in by leadership and stake-holders.
- Companies evaluated their employees by comparing them with the "ideal" employee. Trait appraisal only looks at what employees should be, not at what they should do. When this approach is not properly set, agreed and managed by organizations, self-centered employees might be prone to distort results, falsely representing achievement

of targets that were set in a short-term, narrow fashion. In this case, managing by objectives would be counterproductive.

2.8. Strategies

The term 'Strategy' has been adapted from war and is being increasingly used in business to reflect broad overall objectives and policies of an enterprise. Literally speaking, the term 'Strategy' stands for the war-art of the military general, compelling the enemy to fight as per out chosen terms and conditions.

According to Koontz and O' Donnell, "Strategies must often denote a general programmer of action and deployment of emphasis and resources to attain comprehensive objectives". Strategies are plans made in the light of the plans of the competitors because a modern business institution operates in a competitive environment. They are a useful framework for guiding enterprise thinking and action. A perfect strategy can be built only on perfect knowledge of the plans of others in the industry. This may be done by the management of a firm putting itself in the place of a rival firm and trying to estimate their plans.

2.8.1. Characteristics of Strategy

- It is the right combination of different factors.
- It relates the business organization to the environment.
- It is an action to meet a particular challenge, to solve particular problems or to attain desired objectives.
- Strategy is a means to an end and not an end in itself.
- It is formulated at the top management level.
- It involves assumption of certain calculated risks.

2.8.2. Strategic Planning Process/Strategic Formulation Process

1. **Input to the Organization:** Various Inputs (People, Capital, Management and Technical skills, others) including goals input of claimants (Employees, Consumers, Suppliers, Stockholders, Government, Community and others)need to be elaborated.

2. **Industry Analysis:** Formulation of strategy requires the evaluation of the attractiveness of an industry by analyzing the external environment. The focus should be on the kind of compaction within an industry, the possibility of new firms entering the market, the availability of substitute products or services, the bargaining positions of the suppliers, and buyers or customers.

3. **Enterprise Profile:** Enterprise profile is usually the starting point for determining where the company is and where it should go. Top managers determine the basic purpose of the enterprise and clarify the firm's geographic orientation.

4. **Orientation, Values, and Vision of Executives:** The enterprise profile is shaped by people, especially executives, and their orientation and values are important for formulation the strategy. They set the organizational climate, and they determine the direction of the firm though their vision. Consequently, their values, their preferences, and their attitudes toward risk have to be carefully examined because they have an impact on the strategy.

5. **Mission (Purpose), Major Objectives, and Strategic Intent:** Mission or Purpose is the answer to the question: What is our business? The major Objectives are the end points towards which the activates of the enterprise are directed. Strategic intent is the commitment (obsession) to win in the competitive environment, not only at the top-level but also throughout the organization.

6. **Present and Future External Environment:** The present and future external environment must be assessed in terms of threats and opportunities.

7. **Internal Environment:** Internal Environment should be audited and evaluated with respect to its resources and its weaknesses, and strengths in research and development, production, operation, procurement, marketing and products and services. Other internal factors include, human resources and financial resources as well as the company image, the organization structure and climate, the planning and control system, and relations with customers.

8. **Development of Alternative Strategies:** Strategic alternatives are developed on the basis of an analysis of the external and internal environment. Strategies may be specialize or concentrate. Alternatively, a firm may diversify, extending the operation into new and profitable markets. Other examples of possible strategies are joint ventures, and strategic alliances which may be an appropriate strategy for some firms.

9. **Evaluation and Choice of Strategies:** Strategic choices must be considered in the light of the risk involved in a particular decision. Some profitable opportunities may not be pursued because a failure in a risky venture could result in bankruptcy of the firm. Another critical element in choosing a strategy is timing. Even the best product may fail if it is introduced to the market at an inappropriate time.

10. **Medium/Short Range Planning, Implementation through Reengineering the Organization Structure, Leadership and Control:** Implementation of the Strategy often requires reengineering the organization, staffing the organization structure and providing leadership. Controls must also be installed monitoring performance against plans.

11. **Consistency Testing and Contingency Planning:** The last key aspect of the strategic planning process is the testing for consistency and preparing for contingency plans.

2.8.3.   Types of Strategies

According to Michel Porter, the strategies can be classified into three types. They are

a)   Cost leadership strategy

b)   Differentiation strategy

c)   Focus strategy

The following table illustrates Porter's generic strategies in the Fig 2.2.

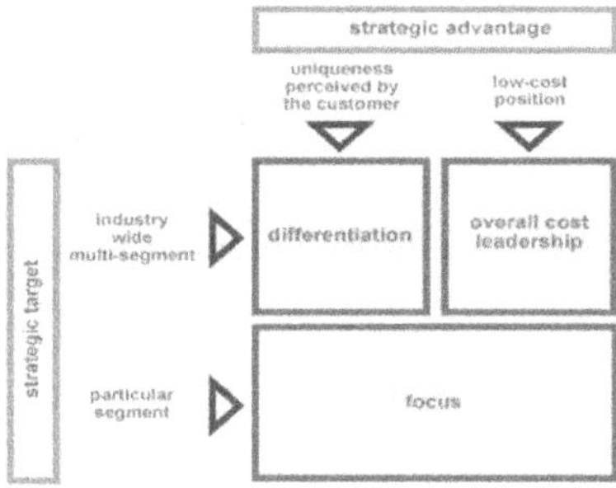

Fig 2.2: Strategies

a.   Cost Leadership Strategy

This generic strategy calls for being the low cost producer in an industry for a given level of quality. The firm sells its products either at average industry prices to earn a profit higher than that of rivals, or below the average industry prices to gain market share. In the event of a price war, the firm can maintain some profitability while the competition suffers losses. Even without a price war, as the industry matures and prices decline, the firms that can produce more cheaply will remain profitable for a longer period of time. The cost leadership strategy usually targets a broad market. Some of the ways that firms acquire cost advantages are by improving process efficiencies, gaining unique access to a large source of lower cost materials, making optimal outsourcing and vertical integration decisions, or avoiding some costs altogether. If competing firms are unable to lower their costs by a similar amount, the firm may be able to sustain a competitive advantage based on cost leadership.

Firms that succeed in cost leadership often have the following internal strengths:

- Access to the capital required to make a significant investment in production assets; this investment represents a barrier to entry that many firms may not overcome.
- Skill in designing products for efficient manufacturing, for example, having a small component count to shorten the assembly process.
- High level of expertise in manufacturing process engineering.
- Efficient distribution channels.

Each generic strategy has its risks, including the low-cost strategy. For example, other firms may be able to lower their costs as well. As technology improves, the competition may be able to leapfrog the production capabilities, thus eliminating the competitive advantage.

Additionally, several firms following a focus strategy and targeting various narrow markets may be able to achieve an even lower cost within their segments and as a group gain significant market share.

b. *Differentiation Strategy*

A differentiation strategy calls for the development of a product or service that offers unique attributes that are valued by customers and that customers perceive to be better than or different from the products of the competition. The value added by the uniqueness of the product may allow the firm to charge a premium price for it. The firm hopes that the higher price will more than cover the extra costs incurred in offering the unique product. Because of the product's unique attributes, if suppliers increase their prices the firm may be able to pass along the costs to its customers who cannot find substitute products easily. Firms that succeed in a differentiation strategy often have the following internal strengths:

- Access to leading scientific research.
- Highly skilled and creative product development team.
- Strong sales team with the ability to successfully communicate the perceived strengths of the product.
- Corporate reputation for quality and innovation.

The risks associated with a differentiation strategy include imitation by competitors and changes in customer tastes. Additionally, various firms pursuing focus strategies may be able to achieve even greater differentiation in their market segments.

c. *Focus Strategy*

The focus strategy concentrates on a narrow segment and within that segment attempts to achieve either a cost advantage or differentiation. The premise is that the needs of the group can be better serviced by focusing entirely on it. A firm using a focus strategy often enjoys a high degree of customer loyalty, and this entrenched loyalty discourages other firms from competing directly.

Because of their narrow market focus, firms pursuing a focus strategy have lower volumes and therefore less bargaining power with their suppliers. However, firms pursuing a differentiation-focused strategy may be able to pass higher costs on to customers since close substitute products do not exist.

Firms that succeed in a focus strategy are able to tailor a broad range of product development strengths to a relatively narrow market segment that they know very well. Some risks of focus strategies include imitation and changes in the target segments. Furthermore, it may be fairly easy for a broad-market cost leader to adapt its product in order to compete directly. Finally, other focusers may be able to carve out sub-segments that they can serve even better.

2.8.4. *A Combination of Generic Strategies*

These generic strategies are not necessarily compatible with one another. If a firm attempts to achieve an advantage on all fronts, in this attempt it may achieve no advantage at all. For example, if a firm differentiates itself by supplying very high quality products, it risks undermining that quality if it seeks to become a cost leader. Even if the quality did not suffer, the firm would risk projecting a confusing image. For this reason, Michael Porter argued that to be successful over the long-term, a firm must select only one of these three generic strategies. Otherwise, with more than one single generic strategy the firm will be "stuck in the middle" and will not achieve a competitive advantage.

Porter argued that firms that are able to succeed at multiple strategies often do so by creating separate business units for each strategy. By separating the strategies into different units having different policies and even different cultures, a corporation is less likely to become "stuck in the middle."

However, there exists a viewpoint that a single generic strategy is not always best because within the same product customers often seek multi-dimensional satisfactions such as a combination of quality, style, convenience, and price. There have been cases in which high quality producers faithfully followed a single strategy and then suffered greatly when another firm entered the market with a lower-quality product that better met the overall needs of the customers.

2.9.   Policies

Policies are general statements or understandings that guide managers' thinking in decision making. They usually do not require action but are intended to guide managers in their commitment to the decision they ultimately make.

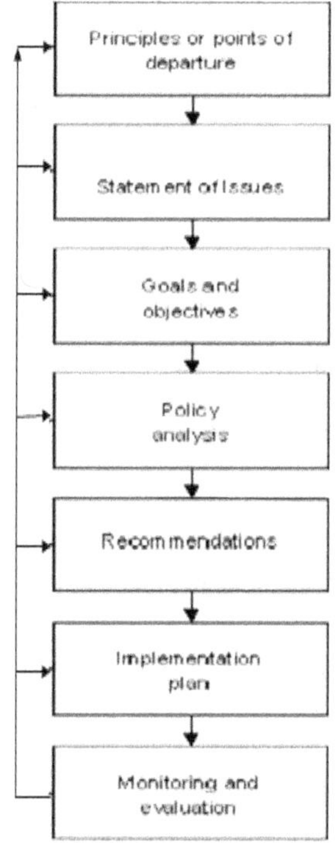

Fig 2.3: Policies

The first step in the process of policy formulation, as shown in the Fig 2.3 below, is to capture the values or principles that will guide the rest of the process and form the basis on which to produce a statement of issues. The statement of issues involves identifying the opportunities and constraints affecting the local housing market, and is to be produced by thoroughly analyzing the housing market. The kit provides the user with access to a housing data base to facilitate this analysis.

The statement of issues will provide the basis for the formulation of a set of housing goals and objectives, designed to address the problems identified and to exploit the opportunities which present themselves.

The next step is to identify and analyze the various policy options which can be applied to achieve the set of goals and objectives. The options available to each local government will depend on local circumstances as much as the broader context and each local authority will have to develop its own unique approach to addressing the housing needs of its residents. An implementation program for realizing the policy recommendations must then be prepared, addressing budgetary and programming requirements, and allocating roles and responsibilities. Finally, the implementation of the housing strategy needs to be systematically monitored and evaluated against the stated goals and objectives, and the various components of the strategy modified or strengthened, as required.

At each step of the way, each component of the strategy needs to be discussed and debated, and a public consultation process engaged in. The extent of consultation and the participants involved will vary with each step.

2.9.1. *Essentials of Policy Formulation*

The essentials of policy formation may be listed as below:

- A policy should be definite, positive and clear. It should be understood by everyone in the organization.
- A policy should be translatable into the practices.
- A policy should be flexible and at the same time have a high degree of permanency.
- A policy should be formulated to cover all reasonable anticipatable conditions.
- A policy should be founded upon facts and sound judgment.
- A policy should conform to economic principles, statutes and regulations.
- A policy should be a general statement of the established rule.

Importance of Policies

Policies are useful for the following reasons:

- They provide guides to thinking and action and provide support to the subordinates.
- They delimit the area within which a decision is to be made.
- They save time and effort by pre-deciding problems and
- They permit delegation of authority to mangers at the lower levels.

2.10. Decision Making

The word decision has been derived from the Latin word "decidere" which means "cutting off". Thus, decision involves cutting off of alternatives between those that are desirable and those that are not desirable. In the words of George R. Terry, "Decision-making is the selection based on some criteria from two or more possible alternatives".

Characteristics of Decision Making

- Decision making implies that there are various alternatives and the most desirable alternative is chosen to solve the problem or to arrive at expected results.
- The decision-maker has freedom to choose an alternative.
- Decision-making may not be completely rational but may be judge mental and emotional.
- Decision-making is goal-oriented.
- Decision-making is a mental or intellectual process because the final decision is made by the decision-maker.
- A decision may be expressed in words or may be implied from behavior.
- Choosing from among the alternative courses of operation implies uncertainty about the final result of each possible course of operation.
- Decision making is rational. It is taken only after a thorough analysis and reasoning and weighing the consequences of the various alternatives.

2.10.1. Types of Decisions

a) Programmed and Non-Programmed Decisions: Herbert Simon has grouped organizational decisions into two categories based on the procedure followed. They are:

i.   *Programmed Decisions*

Programmed decisions are routine and repetitive and are made within the framework of organizational policies and rules. These policies and rules are established well in advance to solve recurring problems in the organization. Programmed decisions have short-run impact. They are, generally, taken at the lower level of management.

ii.   *Non-Programmed Decisions*

Non-programmed decisions are decisions taken to meet non-repetitive problems. Non-programmed decisions are relevant for solving unique/ unusual problems in which various alternatives cannot be decided in advance. A common feature of non-programmed decisions is that they are novel and non-recurring and therefore, readymade solutions are not available. Since these decisions are of high importance and have long-term consequences, they are made by top level management.

b) Strategic and Tactical Decisions: Organizational decisions may also be classified as strategic or tactical.

i.   *Strategic Decisions*

Basic decisions or strategic decisions are decisions which are of crucial importance. Strategic decisions a major choice of actions concerning allocation of resources and contribution to the achievement of organizational objectives. Decisions like plant location, product diversification, entering into new markets, selection of channels of distribution, capital expenditure etc are examples of basic or strategic decisions.

ii.   *Tactical Decisions*

Routine decisions or tactical decisions are decisions which are routine and repetitive. They are derived out of strategic decisions. The various features of a tactical decision are as follows:

- Tactical decision relates to day-to-day operation of the organization and has to be taken very frequently.
- Tactical decision is mostly a programmed one. Therefore, the decision can be made within the context of these variables.
- The outcome of tactical decision is of short-term nature and affects a narrow part of the organization.
- The authority for making tactical decisions can be delegated to lower level managers because: first, the impact of tactical decision is narrow and of short-term nature and Second, by delegating authority for such decisions to lower-level managers, higher level managers are free to devote more time on strategic decisions.

2.10.2. Decision Making Process

The decision making process is presented in the figure 2.4 below:

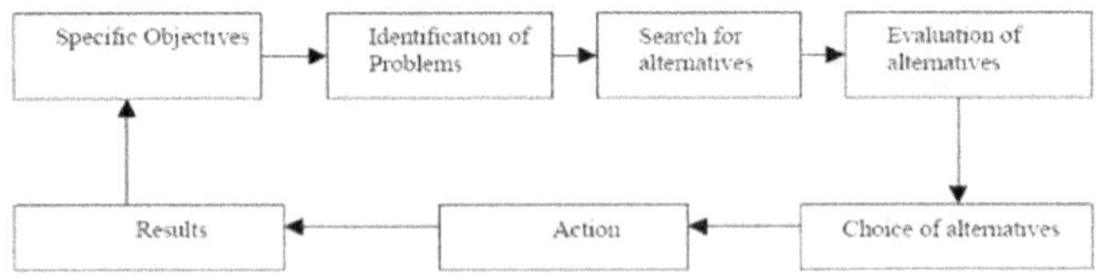

Fig 2.4: Decision Making Process

1. **Specific Objective:** The need for decision making arises in order to achieve certain specific objectives. The starting point in any analysis of decision making involves the determination of whether a decision needs to be made.

2. **Problem Identification:** A problem is a felt need, a question which needs a solution. In the words of Joseph L Massie "A good decision is dependent upon the recognition of the right problem". The objective of problem identification is that if the problem is precisely and specifically identifies, it will provide a clue in finding a possible solution. A problem can be identified clearly, if managers go through diagnosis and analysis of the problem.

   Diagnosis: Diagnosis is the process of identifying a problem from its signs and symptoms. A symptom is a condition or set of conditions that indicates the existence of a problem. Diagnosing the real problem implies knowing the gap between what is and what ought to be, identifying the reasons for the gap and understanding the problem in relation to higher objectives of the organization.

   Analysis: Diagnosis gives rise to analysis. Analysis of a problem requires:
   - Who would make decision?
   - What information would be needed?
   - From where the information is available?
   - Analysis helps managers to gain an insight into the problem

3. **Search for Alternatives:** A problem can be solved in several ways; however, all the ways cannot be equally satisfying. Therefore, the decision maker must try to find out the various alternatives available in order to get the most satisfactory result of a decision. A decision maker can use several sources for identifying alternatives:
   - His own past experiences
   - Practices followed by others and
   - Using creative techniques.

4. **Evaluation of Alternatives:** After the various alternatives are identified, the next step is to evaluate them and select the one that will meet the choice criteria, /the decision maker must check proposed alternatives against limits, and if an alternative does not meet them, he can discard it. Having narrowed down the alternatives which require serious consideration, the decision maker will go for evaluating how each alternative may contribute towards the objective supposed to be achieved by implementing the decision.

5. **Choice of Alternative:** The evaluation of various alternatives presents a clear picture as to how each one of them contribute to the objectives under question. A comparison is made among the likely outcomes of various alternatives and the best one is chosen.

6. **Action:** Once the alternative is selected, it is put into action. The actual process of decision making ends with the choice of an alternative through which the objectives can be achieved.

7. **Results:** When the decision is put into action, it brings certain results. These results must correspond with objectives, the starting point of decision process, if good decision has been made and implemented properly. Thus, results provide indication whether decision making and its implementation is proper.

Characteristics of Effective Decisions

An effective decision is one which should contain three aspects. These aspects are given below:

- **Action Orientation:** Decisions are action-oriented and are directed towards relevant and controllable aspects of the environment. Decisions should ultimately find their utility in implementation.

- **Goal Direction:** Decision making should be goal-directed to enable the organization to meet its objectives.

- **Effective in Implementation:** Decision making should take into account all the possible factors not only in terms of external context but also in internal context so that a decision can be implemented properly.

2.10.3. Rational Decision Making Model

The Rational Decision Making Model is a model which emerges from Organizational Behavior. The process is one that is logical and follows the orderly path from problem identification through solution. It provides a structured and sequenced approach to decision making. Using such an approach can help to ensure discipline and consistency is built into your decision making process.

The Six-Step Rational Decision-Making Model

1. Define the problem.
2. Identify decision criteria
3. Weight the criteria
4. Generate alternatives
5. Rate each alternative on each criterion
6. Compute the optimal decision.

1. Defining the Problem

This is the initial step of the rational decision making process. First the problem is identied and then defined to get a clear view of the situation.

2. Identify Decision Criteria

Once a decision maker has defined the problem, he or she needs to identify the decision criteria that will be important in solving the problem. In this step, the decision maker is determining what's relevant in making the decision. This step brings the decision maker's interests, values, and personal preferences into the process. Identifying criteria is important because what one person thinks is relevant, another may not. Also keep in mind that any factors not identified in this step are considered as irrelevant to the decision maker.

3. Weight the Criteria

The decision-maker weights the previously identified criteria in order to give them correct priority in the decision.

4. Generate Alternatives

The decision maker generates possible alternatives that could succeed in resolving the problem. No attempt is made in this step to appraise these alternatives, only to list them.

5. Rate Each Alternative on Each Criterion

The decision maker must critically analyze and evaluate each one. The strengths and weakness of each alternative become evident as they compared with the criteria and weights established in second and third steps.

6. Compute the Optimal Decision

Evaluating each alternative against the weighted criteria and selecting the alternative with the highest total score.

2.10.4. Decision Making under Various Conditions

The conditions for making decisions can be divided into three types. Namely

a) Certainty

b) Uncertainty and

c) Risk

Virtually all decisions are made in an environment to at least some uncertainty However; the degree will vary from relative certainty to great uncertainty. There are certain risks involved in making decisions.

a. Certainty

In a situation involving certainty, people are reasonably sure about what will happen when they make a decision. The information is available and is considered to be reliable, and the cause and effect relationships are known.

b. Uncertainty

In a situation of uncertainty, on the other hand, people have only a meager database, they do not know whether or not the data are reliable, and they are very unsure about whether or not the situation may change. Moreover, they cannot evaluate the interactions of the different variables. For example, a corporation that decides to expand its Operation to an unfamiliar country may know little about the country, culture, laws, economic environment, and politics. The political situation may be volatile that even experts cannot predict a possible change in government.

c. Risk

In a situation with risks, factual information may exist, but it may be incomplete. 1o improve decision making One may estimate the objective probability of an outcome by using, for example, mathematical models On the other hand, subjective probability, based on judgment and experience may be used All intelligent decision makers dealing with uncertainty like to know the degree and nature of the risk they are taking in choosing a course of action. One of the deficiencies in using the traditional approaches of operations research for problem solving is that many of the data used in model are merely estimates and others are based on probabilities. The ordinary practice is to have staff specialists conic up with best estimates.

Virtually every decision is based on the interaction of a number of important variables, many of which has e an element of uncertainty but, perhaps, a fairly high degree of probability. Thus, the wisdom of launching a new product might depend on a number of critical variables: the cost of introducing the product, the cost of producing it, the capital investment that will he required, the price that can be set for the product, the size of the potential market, and the share of the total market that it will represent.

Unit III

Organizing

Definition

According to Koontz and O'Donnell, "Organization involves the grouping of activities necessary to accomplish goals and plans, the assignment of these activities to appropriate departments and the provision of authority, delegation and co-ordination." Organization involves division of work among people whose efforts must be co-ordinate to achieve specific objectives and to implement pre-determined strategies.

3.1.   Nature or Characteristics of Organizing

From the study of the various definitions given by different management experts we get the following information about the characteristics or nature of organization.

(1) **Division of Work:** Division of work is the basis of an organization. In other words, there can be no organization without division of work. Under division of work the entire work of business is divided into many departments The work of every department is further sub-divided into sub-works. In this way each individual has to do the saran work repeatedly which gradually makes that person an expert.

(2) **Coordination:** Under organizing different persons are assigned different works but the aim of all these persons happens to be the some - the attainment of the objectives of the enterprise. Organization ensures that the work of all the persons depends on each other's work even though it happens to be different. The work of one person starts from where the work of another person ends. The non-completion of the work of one person affects the work of everybody. Therefore, everybody completes his work in time and does not hinder the work of others. It is thus, clear that it is in the nature of an organization to establish coordination among different works, departments and posts in the enterprise.

(3) **Plurality of Persons:** Organization is a group of many persons who assemble to fulfill a common purpose. A single individual cannot create an organization.

(4) **Common Objectives:** There are various parts of an organization with different functions to perform but all move in the direction of achieving a general objective.

(5) **Well-defined Authority and Responsibility:** Under organization a chain is established between different posts right from the top to the bottom. It is clearly specified as to what will be the authority and responsibility of every post. In other words, every individual working in the organization is given some authority for the efficient work performance and it is also decided simultaneously as to what will be the responsibility of that individual in case of unsatisfactory work performance.

(6) **Organization is a Structure of Relationship:** Relationship between persons working on different posts in the organization is decided. In other words, it is decided as to who will be the superior and who will be the subordinate. Leaving the top level post and the lowest level post everybody is somebody's superior and somebody's subordinate. The person working on the top level post has no superior and the person working on the lowest level post has no subordinate.

(7) **Organization is a Machine of Management:** Organization is considered to be a machine of management because the efficiency of all the functions depends on an effective organization. In the absence of organization no function can be performed in a planned manner. It is appropriate to call organization a machine of management from another point of view. It is that machine in which no part can afford tube ill-fitting or non-functional. In other words, if the division of work is not done properly or posts are not created correctly the whole system of management collapses.

(8) **Organization is a Universal Process:** Organization is needed both in business and nonbusiness organizations. Not only this, organization will be needed where two or mom than two people work jointly. Therefore, organization has the quality of universality. (9) Organization is a Dynamic Process: Organization is related to people and the knowledge and experience of the people undergo a change. The impact of this change affects the various functions of the organizations. Thus, organization is not a process that can be decided for all times to come but it undergoes changes according to the needs. The example in this case can be the creation or abolition of a new post according to the need.

3.2.   Import ANCEORADV ant AGESOFORGANIZING

Organization is an instrument that defines relations among different people which helps them to understand as in who happens to be their superior and who is their subordinate. This information helps in fixing responsibility and developing coordination. In such circumstances the objectives of the organization can be easily achieved. That is why, it is said that Organization Is a mechanism of management. In addition to that it helps in the other functions of management like planning, staffing, leading, controlling, etc. The importance of organization or its merits becomes clear from the following facts,

1. **Increase In Managerial Efficiency:** A good and balanced organization helps the managers to increase their efficiency. Managers, through the medium of organization, make a proper distribution of the whole work among different people according to their ability.

2. **Proper Utilization of Resources:** Through the medium of organization optimum utilization of all the available human and material resources of an enterprise becomes possible. Work is allotted to every individual according to his ability and capacity and conditions ant created to enable him to utilize his ability to the maximum extent. For example, if an employee possesses the knowledge of modem machinery but the modem machinery is not available in the organization, in that case, efforts are made to make available the modem machinery.

3. **Sound Communication Possible:** Communication is essential for taking the right decision at the right time. However, the establishment of a good communication system is possible only through an organization. In an organization the time of communication is decided so that all the useful information reaches the officers concerned which, in turn, helps the decision-making.

4. **Facilitates Coordination:** In order to attain successfully the objectives of the organization, coordination among various activities in the organization is essential. Organization is the only medium which makes coordination possible. Under organization the division of work is made in such a manner as to make all the activities complementary to each other increasing their interdependence. Inter-dependence gives rise to the establishment of relations which, in turn, increases coordination.

5. **Increase in Specialization:** Under organization the whole work is divided into different parts. Competent persons are appointed to handle all the sub-works and by handling a particular work repeatedly they become specialists. This enables them to have maximum work performance in the minimum time while the organization gets the benefit of specialization.

6. **Helpful in Expansion:** A good organization helps the enterprise in facing competition. When an enterprise starts making available good quality product at cheap rates, it increases the demand for its products. In order to meet the increasing demand for its products and organization has to expand its business. On the other hand, a good

organization has an element of flexibility which far from impeding the expansion work encourages it.

3.3.   Organizing Process

Organization is the process of establishing relationship among the members of the enterprise. The relationships are created in terms of authority and responsibility. To organize is to harmonize, coordinate or arrange in a logical and orderly manner. Each member in the organization is assigned a specific responsibility or duty to perform and is granted the corresponding authority to perform his duty. The managerial function of organizing consists in making a rational division of work into groups of activities and tying together the positions representing grouping of activities so as to achieve a rational, well coordinated and orderly structure for the accomplishment of work. According to Louis A Allen, "Organizing involves identification and grouping the activities to be performed and dividing them among the individuals and creating authority and responsibility relationships among them for the accomplishment of organizational objectives."

The various steps involved in this process are:

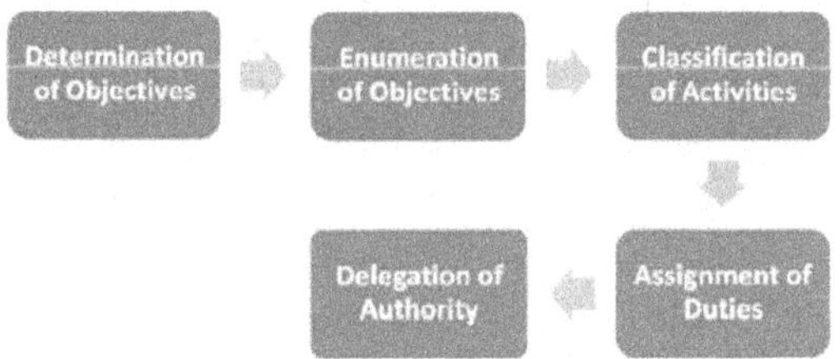

Fig 3.1: Organizing Process

a) Determination of Objectives

It is the first step in building up an organization. Organization is always related to certain objectives. Therefore, it is essential for the management to identify the objectives before starting any activity. Organization structure is built on the basis of the objectives of the enterprise. That means, the structure of the organization can be determined by the management only after knowing the objectives to be accomplished through the organization. This step helps the management not only in framing the organization structure but also in achieving the enterprise objectives with minimum cost and efforts. Determination of objectives will consist in deciding as to why the proposed organization is to be set up and, therefore, what will be the nature of the work to be accomplished through the organization.

b) *Enumeration of Objectives*

If the members of the group are to pool their efforts effectively, there must be proper division of the major activities. The first step in organizing group effort is the division of the total job into essential activities. Each job should be properly classified and grouped. This will enable the people to know what is expected of them as members of the group and will help in avoiding duplication of efforts. For example, the work of an industrial concern may be divided into the following major functions-production, financing, personnel, sales, purchase, etc.

c) *Classification of Activities*

The next step will be to classify activities according to similarities and common purposes and functions and taking the human and material resources into account. Then, closely related and similar activities are grouped into divisions and departments and the departmental activities are further divided into sections.

d) *Assignment of Duties*

Here, specific job assignments are made to different subordinates for ensuring a certainty of work performance. Each individual should be given a specific job to do according to his ability and made responsible for that. He should also be given the adequate authority to do the job assigned to him. In the words of Kimball and Kimball - "Organization embraces the duties of designating the departments and the personnel that are to carry on the work, defining their functions and specifying the relations that are to exist between department and individuals."

e) *Delegation of Authority*

Since so many individuals work in the same organization, it is the responsibility of management to lay down structure of relationship in the organization. Authority without responsibility is a dangerous thing and similarly responsibility without authority is an empty vessel. Everybody should clearly know to whom he is accountable; corresponding to the responsibility authority is delegated to the subordinates for enabling them to show work performance. This will help in the smooth working of the enterprise by facilitating delegation of responsibility and authority.

3.3.1. *Organization Structure*

An organization structure is a framework that allots a particular space for a particular department or an individual and shows its relationship to the other. An organization structure shows the authority and responsibility relationships between the various positions in the organization by showing who reports to whom.

It is an established pattern of relationship among the components of the organization.

March and Simon have stated that-"Organization structure consists simply of those aspects of pattern of behavior in the organization that are relatively stable and change only slowly." The structure of an organization is generally shown on an organization chart. It shows the authority and responsibility relationships between various positions in the organization while designing the organization structure, due attention should be given to the principles of sound organization.

Significance of Organization Structure

- Properly designed organization can help improve teamwork and productivity by providing a framework within which the people can work together most effectively.
- Organization structure determines the location of decision-making in the organization.
- Sound organization structure stimulates creative thinking and initiative among organizational members by providing well defined patterns of authority.
- A sound organization structure facilitates growth of enterprise by increasing its capacity to handle increased level of authority.
- Organization structure provides the pattern of communication and coordination.
- The organization structure helps a member to know what his role is and how it relates to other roles.

3.3.2. Principles of Organization Structure

Modern organizational structures have evolved from several organizational theories, which have identified certain principles as basic to any organization structure.

a. Line and Staff Relationships

Line authority refers to the scalar chain, or to the superior-subordinate linkages, that extend throughout the hierarchy (Koontz, O'Donnell and Weihrich). Line employees are responsible for achieving the basic or strategic objectives of the organization, while staff plays a supporting role to line employees and provides services. The relationship between line and staff is crucial in organizational structure, design and efficiency. It is also an important aid to information processing and coordination.

b. *Departmentalization*

Departmentalization is a process of horizontal clustering of different types of functions and activities on any one level of the hierarchy. Departmentalization is conventionally based on purpose, product, process, function, personal things and place.

c. *Span of Control*

This refers to the number of specialized activities or individuals supervised by one person. Deciding the span of control is important for coordinating different types of activities effectively.

d. *De-centralization and Centralization*

De-centralization refers to decision making at lower levels in the hierarchy of authority. In contrast, decision making in a centralized type of organizational structure is at higher levels. The degree of centralization and de-centralization depends on the number of levels of hierarchy, degree of coordination, specialization and span of control.

Every organizational structure contains both centralization and de-centralization, but to varying degrees. The extent of this can be determined by identifying how much of the decision making is concentrated at the top and how much is delegated to lower levels. Modern organizational structures show a strong tendency towards de-centralization.

3.3.3. *Formal and Informal Organization*

The formal organization refers to the structure of jobs and positions with clearly defined functions and relationships as prescribed by the top management. This type of organization is built by the management to realize objectives of an enterprise and is bound by rules, systems and procedures. Everybody is assigned a certain responsibility for the performance of the given task and given the required amount of authority for carrying it out. Informal organization, which does not appear on the organization chart, supplements the formal organization in achieving organizational goals effectively and efficiently. The working of informal groups and leaders is not as simple as it may appear to be. Therefore, it is obligatory for every manager to study thoroughly the working pattern of informal relationships in the organization and to use them for
achieving organizational objectives.

Formal Organization

Chester I Bernard defines formal organization as -"a system of consciously coordinated activities or forces of two or more persons. It refers to the structure of well-defined jobs, each bearing a definite measure of authority, responsibility and accountability." The essence of formal organization is conscious common purpose and comes into being when persons-

i.   Are able to communicate with each other

ii.   Are willing to act and

iii.   Share a purpose.

The formal organization is built around four key pillars. They are:

- Division of labor
- Scalar and functional processes
- Structure and
- Span of control

Thus, a formal organization is one resulting from planning where the pattern of structure has already been determined by the top management.

Characteristic Features of Formal Organization

- Formal organization structure is laid down by the top management to achieve organizational goals.
- Formal organization prescribes the relationships amongst the people working in the organization.
- The organization structures is consciously designed to enable the people of the organization to work together for accomplishing the common objectives of the enterprise
- Organization structure concentrates on the jobs to be performed and not the individuals who are to perform jobs.
- In a formal organization, individuals are fitted into jobs and positions and work as per the managerial decisions. Thus, the formal relations in the organization arise from the pattern of responsibilities that are created by the management.
- A formal organization is bound by rules, regulations and procedures.
- In a formal organization, the position, authority, responsibility and accountability of each level are clearly defined.
- Organization structure is based on division of labor and specialization to achieve efficiency in operations.

- A formal organization is deliberately impersonal. The organization does not take into consideration the sentiments of organizational members.
- The authority and responsibility relationships created by the organization structure are to be honored by everyone.
- In a formal organization, coordination proceeds according to the prescribed pattern.

Advantages of Formal Organization

- The formal organization structure concentrates on the jobs to be performed. It, therefore, makes everybody responsible for a given task.
- A formal organization is bound by rules, regulations and procedures. It thus ensures law and order in the organization.
- The organization structure enables the people of the organization to work together for accomplishing the common objectives of the enterprise

Disadvantages or Criticisms of Formal Organization

- The formal organization does not take into consideration the sentiments of organizational members.
- The formal organization does not consider the goals of the individuals. It is designed to achieve the goals of the organization only.
- The formal organization is bound by rigid rules, regulations and procedures. This makes the achievement of goals difficult.

Informal Organization

Informal organization refers to the relationship between people in the organization based on personal attitudes, emotions, prejudices, likes, dislikes etc. an informal organization is an organization which is not established by any formal authority, but arises from the personal and social relations of the people. These relations are not developed according to procedures and regulations laid down in the formal organization structure; generally large formal groups give rise to small informal or social groups. These groups may be based on same taste, language, culture or some other factor. These groups are not pre-planned, but they develop automatically within the organization according to its environment.

Characteristics Features of Informal Organization

- Informal organization is not established by any formal authority. It is unplanned and arises spontaneously.
- Informal organizations reflect human relationships. It arises from the personal and social relations amongst the people working in the organization.
- Formation of informal organizations is a natural process. It is not based on rules, regulations and procedures.
- The inter-relations amongst the people in an informal organization cannot be shown in an organization chart.
- In the case of informal organization, the people cut across formal channels of communications and communicate amongst themselves.
- The membership of informal organizations is voluntary. It arises spontaneously and not by deliberate or conscious efforts.
- Membership of informal groups can be overlapping as a person may be member of a number of informal groups.
- Informal organizations are based on common taste, problem, language, religion, culture, etc. it is influenced by the personal attitudes, emotions, whims, likes and dislikes etc. of the people in the organization.

Benefits of Informal Organization

- It blends with the formal organization to make it more effective.
- Many things which cannot be achieved through formal organization can be achieved through informal organization.
- The presence of informal organization in an enterprise makes the managers plan and act more carefully.
- Informal organization acts as a means by which the workers achieve a sense of security and belonging. It provides social satisfaction to group members.
- An informal organization has a powerful influence on productivity and job satisfaction.
- The informal leader lightens the burden of the formal manager and tries to fill in the gaps in the manager's ability.
- Informal organization helps the group members to attain specific personal objectives.
- Informal organization is the best means of employee communication. It is very fast.

- Informal organization gives psychological satisfaction to the members. It acts as a safety valve for the emotional problems and frustrations of the workers of the organization because they get a platform to express their feelings.
- It serves as an agency for social control of human behavior.

3.3.4. *Differences between Formal and Informal Organization*

Formal Organization	Informal Organization
1. Formal organization is established with the explicit aim of achieving well-defined goals.	1. Informal organization springs on its own. Its goals are ill defined and intangible.
2. Formal organization is bound together by authority relationships among members. A hierarchical structure is created,constituting top management, middle management and supervisory management.	2. Informal organization is characterized by a generalized sort of power relationships. Power in informal organization has bases other than rational legal right.
3. Formal organization recognizes certain tasks which are to be carried out to achieve its goals.	3. Informal organization does not have any well-defined tasks.
4. The roles and relationships of people in formal organization are impersonally defined	4. In informal organization the relationships among people are interpersonal.
5. In formal organization, much emphasis is placed on efficiency, discipline, conformity, consistency and control.	5. Informal organization is characterized by relative freedom, spontaneity, by relative freedom, spontaneity, homeliness and
6. In formal organization, the social and psychological needs and interests of members of the organization get little attention.	6. In informal organization the socio psychological needs, interests and aspirations of members get priority.
7. The communication system in formal organization follows certain pre-determined patterns and paths.	7. In informal organization, the communication pattern is haphazard,
8. Formal organization is relatively slow to respond and adapt to changing situations and realities.	8. Informal organization is dynamic and very vigilant. It is sensitive to its surroundings.

3.4. Line and Staff Authority

In an organization, the line authority flows from top to bottom and the staff authority is exercised by the specialists over the line managers who advise them on important matters. These specialists stand ready with their specialty to serve line mangers as and when their services are called for, to collect information and to give help which will enable the line officials to carry out their activities better. The staff officers do not have any power of command in the organization as they are employed to provide expert advice to the line officers. The 'line' maintains discipline and stability; the 'staff provides expert information. The line gets out the production, the staffs carries on the research, planning, scheduling, establishing of standards and recording of performance. The authority by which the staff performs these functions is delegated by the line and the performance must be acceptable to the line before action is taken.

The following figure depicts the line and staff authority:

3.4.1. Types of Staff

The staff position established as a measure of support for the line managers may take the following forms

1. **Personal Staff:** Here the staff official is attached as a personal assistant or adviser to the line manager. For example, Assistant to managing director.
2. **Specialized Staff:** Such staff acts as the fountainhead of expertise in specialized areas like R & D, personnel, accounting etc.
3. **General Staff:** This category of staff consists of a set of experts in different areas who are meant to advise and assist the top management on matters called for expertise. For example, Financial advisor, technical advisor etc.

Features of Line and Staff Organization

- Under this system, there are line officers who have authority and command over the subordinates and are accountable for the tasks entrusted to them. The staff officers are specialists who offer expert advice to the line officers to perform their tasks efficiently.
- Under this system, the staff officers prepare the plans and give advice to the line officers and the line officers execute the plan with the help of workers.
- The line and staff organization is based on the principle of specialization.

Advantages

- It brings expert knowledge to bear upon management and operating problems. Thus, the line managers get the benefit of specialized knowledge of staff specialists at various levels.
- The expert advice and guidance given by the staff officers to the line officers benefit the entire organization.
- As the staff officers look after the detailed analysis of each important managerial activity, it relieves the line managers of the botheration of concentrating on specialized functions.
- Staff specialists help the line managers in taking better decisions by providing expert advice. Therefore, there will be sound managerial decisions under this system.
- It makes possible the principle of undivided responsibility and authority, and at the same time permits staff specialization. Thus, the organization takes advantage of functional organization while maintaining the unity of command.

- It is based upon planned specialization.
- Line and staff organization has greater flexibility, in the sense that new specialized activities can be added to the line activities without disturbing the line procedure.

Disadvantages

- Unless the duties and responsibilities of the staff members are clearly indicated by charts and manuals, there may be considerable confusion throughout the organization as to the functions and positions of staff members with relation to the line supervisors.
- There is generally a conflict between the line and staff executives. The line managers feel that staff specialists do not always give right type of advice, and staff officials generally complain that their advice is not properly attended to.
- Line managers sometimes may resent the activities of staff members, feeling that prestige and influence of line managers suffer from the presence of the specialists.
- The staff experts may be ineffective because they do not get the authority to implement their recommendations.
- This type of organization requires the appointment of large number of staff officers or experts in addition to the line officers. As a result, this system becomes quite expensive.
- Although expert information and advice are available, they reach the workers through the officers and thus run the risk of misunderstanding and misinterpretation.

3.5.   Departmentation by Different Strategies

It is refers to the process of grouping activities into departments. Departmentation is the process of grouping of work activities into departments, divisions, and other homogenous units.

Key Factors in Departmentation.

- It should facilitate control.
- It should ensure proper coordination.
- It should take into consideration the benefits of specialization.
- It should not result in excess cost.
- It should give due consideration to Human Aspects.

Departmentation takes place in various patterns like departmentation by functions, products, customers, geographic location, process, and its combinations.

a. Functional Departmentation

Functional departmentation is the process of grouping activities by functions performed. Activities can be grouped according to function (work being done) to pursue economies of scale by placing employees with shared skills and knowledge into departments for example human resources, finance, production, and marketing. Functional departmentation can be used in all types of organizations.

Advantages

- Advantage of specialization
- Easy control over functions
- Pinpointing training needs of manager
- It is very simple process of grouping activities.

Disadvantages

- Lack of responsibility for the end result
- Overspecialization or lack of general management
- It leads to increase conflicts and coordination problems among departments.

b. Product Departmentation

Product departmentation is the process of grouping activities by product line. Tasks can also be grouped according to a specific product or service, thus placing all activities related to the product or the service under one manager. Each major product area in the corporation is under the authority of a senior manager who is specialist in, and is responsible for, everything related to the product line. Dabur India Limited is the India's largest Ayurvedic medicine manufacturer is an example of company that uses product departmentation. Its structure is based on its varied product lines which include Home care, Health care, Personal care and Foods.

Advantages

- It ensures better customer service
- Unprofitable products may be easily determined
- It assists in development of all around managerial talent
- Makes control effective
- It is flexible and new product line can be added easily.

Disadvantages

- It is expensive as duplication of service functions occurs in various product divisions
- Customers and dealers have to deal with different persons for complaint and information of different products.

c. *Customer Departmentation*

Customer departmentation is the process of grouping activities on the basis of common customers or types of customers. Jobs may be grouped according to the type of customer served by the organization. The assumption is that customers in each department have a common set of problems and needs that can best be met by specialists. UCO is the one of the largest commercial banks of India is an example of company that uses customer departmentation. Its structure is based on various services which includes Home loans, Business loans, Vehicle loans and Educational loans.

Advantages

- It focused on customers who are ultimate suppliers of money
- Better service to customer having different needs and tastes
- Development in general managerial skills

Disadvantages

- Sales being the exclusive field of its application, co-ordination may appear difficult between sales function and other enterprise functions.
- Specialized sales staff may become idle with the downward movement of sales to any specified group of customers.

d. *Geographic Departmentation*

Geographic departmentation is the process of grouping activities on the basis of territory. If an organization's customers are geographically dispersed, it can group jobs based on geography. For example, the organization structure of Coca-Cola Ltd has reflected the company's operation in various geographic areas such as Central North American group, Western North American group, Eastern North American group and European group

Advantages

- Help to cater to the needs of local people more satisfactorily.
- It facilitates effective control
- Assists in development of all-round managerial skills

Disadvantages

- Communication problem between head office and regional office due to lack of means of communication at some location
- Coordination between various divisions may become difficult.
- Distance between policy framers and executors
- It leads to duplication of activities which may cost higher.

e. Process Departmentation

Geographic departmentation is the process of grouping activities on the basis of product or service or customer flow. Because each process requires different skills, process departmentation allows homogenous activities to be categorized. For example, Bowater Thunder Bay, a Canadian company that harvests trees and processes wood into newsprint and pulp. Bowater has three divisions namely tree cutting, chemical processing, and finishing (which makes newsprint).

Departmentation by Process: Advantages

- Oriented towards end result.
- Professional identification is maintained.
- Pinpoints product-profit responsibility.

Disadvantages

- Conflict in organization authority exists.
- Possibility of disunity of command.
- Requires managers effective in human relation.

f. Martix Departmentation

The Matrix departmentation is explained in the following Fig 3.2.

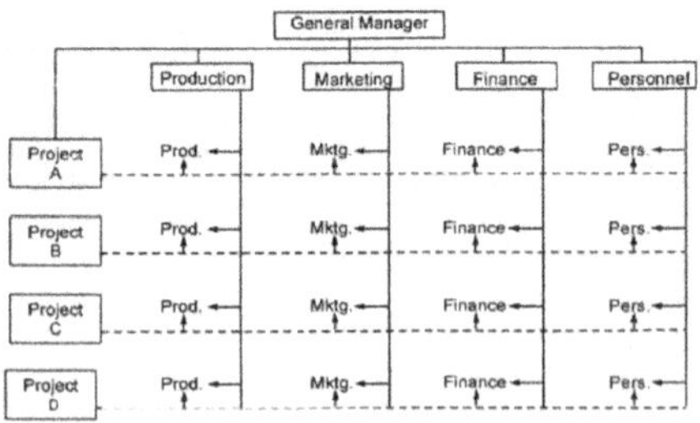

Fig 3.2: Martix Departmentation

In actual practice, no single pattern of grouping activities is applied in the organization structure with all its levels. Different bases are used in different segments of the enterprise. Composite or hybrid method forms the common basis for classifying activities rather than one particular method. One of the mixed forms of organization is referred to as matrix or grid organization's According to the situations, the patterns of Organizing varies from case to case. The form of structure must reflect the tasks, goals and technology if the originations the type of people employed and the environmental conditions that it faces. It is not unusual to see firms that utilize the function and project organization combination. The same is true for process and project as well as other combinations. For instance, a large hospital could have an accounting department, surgery department, marketing department, and a satellite center project team that make up its organizational structure.

Advantages

- Efficiently manage large, complex tasks.
- Effectively carry out large, complex tasks.

Disadvantages

- Requires high levels of coordination.
- Conflict between bosses.
- Requires high levels of management skills.

3.6. Span of Control

Span of Control means the number of subordinates that can be managed efficiently and effectively by a superior in an organization. It suggests how the relations are designed between a superior and a subordinate in an organization.

Factors Affecting Span of Control

a) Capacity of Superior: Different ability and capacity of leadership, communication affect management of subordinates.

b) Capacity of Subordinates: Efficient and trained subordinates affects the degree of span of management.

c) Nature of Work: Different types of work require different patterns of management.

d) Degree of Centralization or Decentralization:Degree of centralization or decentralization affects the span of management by affecting the degree of involvement of the superior in decision making.

e) Degree of Planning: Plans which can provide rules, procedures in doing the work higher would be the degree of span of management.

f) Communication Techniques: Pattern of communication, its means, and media affect the time requirement in managing subordinates and consequently span of management.

g) Use of Staff Assistance: Use of Staff assistance in reducing the work load of managers enables them to manage more number of subordinates,

h) Supervision of others: If subordinate receives supervision form several other personnel besides his direct supervisor. In such a case, the work load of direct superior is reduced and he can supervise more number of persons.

Span of Control is of Two Types

1. **Narrow span of control:** Narrow Span of control means a single manager or supervisor oversees few subordinates. This gives rise to a tall organizational structure.

Advantages

- Close supervision
- Close control of subordinates
- Fast communication

Disadvantages

- Too much control
- Many levels of management
- High costs
- Excessive distance between lowest level and highest level

2. **Wide span of control:** Wide span of control means a single manager or supervisor oversees a large number of subordinates. This gives rise to a flat organizational structure.

Advantages

- More Delegation of Authority.
- Development of Managers.
- Clear policies.

Disadvantages

- Overloaded supervisors.
- Danger of superiors loss of control.
- Requirement of highly trained managerial personnel.
- Block in decision making.

3.7. Centralization and Decentralization

3.7.1. Centralization

It is the process of transferring and assigning decision-making authority to higher levels of an organizational hierarchy. The span of control of top managers is relatively broad, and there are relatively many tiers in the organization.

Characteristics

- Philosophy/emphasis on: top-down control, leadership, vision, strategy.
- Decision-making: strong, authoritarian, visionary, charismatic.
- Organizational change: shaped by top, vision of leader.
- Execution: decisive, fast, coordinated. Able to respond quickly to major issues and changes.
- Uniformity. Low risk of dissent or conflicts between parts of the organization.

Advantages of Centralization

- Provide Power and prestige for manager
- Promote uniformity of policies, practices and decisions
- Minimal extensive controlling procedures and practices
- Minimize duplication of function

Disadvantages of Centralization

- Neglected functions for mid Level, and less motivated beside personnel.
- Nursing supervisor functions as a link officer between nursing director and first-line management.

3.7.2. Decentralization

It is the process of transferring and assigning decision-making authority to lower levels of an organizational hierarchy. The span of control of top managers is relatively small, and there are relatively few tears in the organization, because there is more autonomy in the lower ranks.

Characteristics

- Philosophy / emphasis on: bottom-up, political, cultural and learning dynamics.
- Decision-making: democratic, participative, detailed.
- Organizational change: emerging from interactions, organizational dynamics.
- Execution: evolutionary, emergent. Flexible to adapt to minor issues and changes.
- Participation, accountability. Low risk of not-invented-here behavior.

Three Forms of Decentralization

1. **De-concentration:** The weakest form of decentralization.Decision making authority is redistributed to lower or regional levels of the same central organization.

2. **Delegation:** A more extensive form of decentralization. Through delegation the responsibility for decision-making are transferred to semi-autonomous organizations not wholly controlled by the central organization, but ultimately accountable to it.

3. **Devolution:** A third type of decentralization is devolution. The authority for decision making is transferred completely to autonomous organizational units.

Advantages of Decentralization

- Raise morale and promote interpersonal relationships
- Relieve from the daily administration
- Bring decision-making close to action
- Develop Second-line managers
- Promote employee's enthusiasm and coordination
- Facilitate actions by lower-level managers

Disadvantages of Decentralization

- Top-level administration may feel it would decrease their status
- Managers may not permit full and maximum utilization of highly qualified personnel
- Increased costs. It requires more managers and large staff
- It may lead to overlapping and duplication of effort

Centralization and Decentralization are two opposite ways to transfer decision-making power and to change the organizational structure of organizations accordingly. There must be a good balance between centralization and decentralization of authority and power. Extreme centralization and decentralization must be avoided.

3.8. Delegation of Authority

A manager alone cannot perform all the tasks assigned to him. In order to meet the targets, the manager should delegate authority. Delegation of Authority means division of authority and powers downwards to the subordinate. Delegation is about entrusting someone else to do parts of your job. Delegation of authority can be defined as subdivision and sub-allocation of powers to the subordinates in order to achieve effective results.

Elements of Delegation

1. **Authority** - in context of a business organization, authority can be defined as the power and right of a person to use and allocate the resources efficiently, to take decisions and to give orders so as to achieve the organizational objectives. Authority must be well-defined. All people who have the authority should know what is the scope of their authority is and they shouldn't misutilize it. Authority is the right to give commands, orders and get the things done. The top level management has greatest authority. Authority always flows from top to bottom. It explains how a superior gets work done from his subordinate by clearly explaining what is expected of him and how he should go about it. Authority should be accompanied with an equal amount of responsibility. Delegating the authority to someone else doesn't imply escaping from accountability. Accountability still rest with the person having the utmost authority.

2. **Responsibility** - is the duty of the person to complete the task assigned to him. A person who is given the responsibility should ensure that he accomplishes the tasks assigned to him. If the tasks for which he was held responsible are not completed, then he should not give explanations or excuses. Responsibility without adequate authority leads to discontent and dissatisfaction among the person. Responsibility flows from bottom to top. The middle level and lower level management holds more responsibility. The person held responsible for a job is answerable for it. If he performs the tasks assigned as expected, he is bound for praises. While if he doesn't accomplish tasks assigned as expected, then also he is answerable for that.

3. **Accountability** - means giving explanations for any variance in the actual performance from the expectations set. Accountability cannot be delegated. For example, if 'A' is given a task with sufficient authority, and 'A' delegates this task to B and asks him to ensure that task is done well, responsibility rest with 'B', but accountability still rest with 'A'. The top level management is most accountable. Being accountable means being innovative as the person will think beyond his scope of job. Accountability ,in short, means being answerable for the end result. Accountability can't be escaped. It arises from responsibility.

3.8.1. Delegation Process

The Various steps involved in delegation are given below.

1. **Allocation of duties** -The delegator first tries to define the task and duties to the subordinate. He also has to define the result expected from the subordinates. Clarity of duty as well as result expected has to be the first step in delegation.

2. **Granting of authority** - Subdivision of authority takes place when a superior divides and shares his authority with the subordinate. It is for this reason; every subordinate should be given enough independence to carry the task given to him by his superiors. The managers at all levels delegate authority and power which is attached to their job positions. The subdivision of powers is very important to get effective results.

3. **Assigning of Responsibility and Accountability** - The delegation process does not end once powers are granted to the subordinates. They at the same time have to be obligatory towards the duties assigned to them. Responsibility is said to be the factor or obligation of an individual to carry out his duties in best of his ability as per the directions of superior. Therefore, it is that which gives effectiveness to authority. At the same time, responsibility is absolute and cannot be shifted.

4. **Creation of accountability** - Accountability, on the others hand, is the obligation of the individual to carry out his duties as per the standards of performance. Therefore, it is said that authority is delegated, responsibility is created and accountability is imposed. Accountability arises out of responsibility and responsibility arises out of authority. Therefore, it becomes important that with every authority position an equal and opposite responsibility should be attached.

Therefore every manager, i.e., the delegator has to follow a system to finish up the delegation process. Equally important is the delegate's role which means his responsibility and accountability is attached with the authority over to here.

3.9. Staffing

Staffing involves filling the positions needed in the organization structure by appointing competent and qualified persons for the job. The staffing process encompasses man power planning, recruitment, selection, and training.

a) Manpower Requirements

Manpower Planning which is also called as Human Resource Planning consists of putting right number of people, right kind of people at the right place, right time, doing the right things for which they are suited for the achievement of goals of the organization. The primary function of man power planning is to analyze and evaluate the human resources available in the organization, and to determine how to obtain the kinds of personnel needed to staff positions ranging from assembly line workers to chief executives.

b) Recruitment

Recruitment is the process of finding and attempting to attract job candidates who are capable of effectively filling job vacancies. Job descriptions and job specifications are important in the recruiting process because they specify the nature of the job and the qualifications required of job candidates.

c) Selection

Selecting a suitable candidate can be the biggest challenge for any organization. The success of an organization largely depends on its staff. Selection of the right candidate builds the foundation of any organization's success and helps in reducing turnovers.

d) Training and Development

Training and Development is a planned effort to facilitate employee learning of job-related behaviors in order to improve employee performance. Experts sometimes distinguish between the terms "training" and "development"; "training" denotes efforts to increase employee skills on present jobs, while "development" refers to efforts oriented toward improvements relevant to future jobs. In practice, though, the distinction is often blurred (mainly because upgrading skills in present jobs usually improves performance in future jobs).

3.9.1. Recruitment Process

Recruitment is the process of finding and attempting to attract job candidates who are capable of effectively filling job vacancies. The recruitment process consists of the following steps

a) Identification of vacancy
b) Preparation of job description and job specification
c) Selection of sources
d) Advertising the vacancy
e) Managing the response

a) Identification of Vacancy

The recruitment process begins with the human resource department receiving requisitions for recruitment from any department of the company. These contain:

- Posts to be filled
- Number of persons
- Duties to be performed
- Qualifications required

b) Preparation of Job Description and Job Specification

A job description is a list of the general tasks, or functions, and responsibilities of a position. It may often include to whom the position reports, specifications such as the qualifications or skills needed by the person in the job, or a salary range. A job specification describes the knowledge, skills, education, experience, and abilities you believe are essential to performing a particular job.

c) Selection of Sources

Every organization has the option of choosing the candidates for its recruitment processes from two kinds of sources: internal and external sources. The sources within the organization itself (like transfer of employees from one department to other, promotions) to fill a position are known as the internal sources of recruitment. Recruitment candidates from all the other sources (like outsourcing agencies etc.) are known as the external sources of the recruitment.

d) Advertising the Vacancy

After choosing the appropriate sources, the vacancy is communicated to the candidates by means of a suitable media such as television, radio, newspaper, internet, direct mail etc.

e) Managing the Response

After receiving an adequate number of responses from job seekers, the sieving process of the resumes begins. This is a very essential step of the recruitment selection process, because selecting the correct resumes that match the job profile, is very important. Naturally, it has to be done rather competently by a person who understands all the responsibilities associated with the designation in its entirety. Candidates with the given skill set are then chosen and further called for interview. Also, the applications of candidates that do not match the present nature of the position but may be considered for future requirements are filed separately and preserved. The recruitment process is immediately followed by the selection process.

3.9.2. *Job Analysis*

It is the process of describing and recording aspects of jobs and specifying the skills and other requirements necessary to perform the job. The outputs of job analysis are

a) Job description
b) Job specification

Job Description

A job description (JD) is a written statement of what the job holder does, how it is done, under what conditions it is done and why it is done. It describes what the job is all about, throwing light on job content, environment and conditions of employment. It is descriptive in nature and defines the purpose and scope of a job. The main purpose of writing a job description is to differentiate the job from other jobs and state its outer limits.

Contents: A job description usually covers the following information:

- Job title: Tells about the job title, code number and the department where it is done.
- Job summary: A brief write-up about what the job is all about.
- Job activities: A description of the tasks done, facilities used, extent of supervisory help, etc.
- Working conditions: The physical environment of job in terms of heat, light, noise and other hazards.
- Social environment: Size of work group and interpersonal interactions required to do the job.

Job Specification

Job specification summarizes the human characteristics needed for satisfactory job completion. It tries to describe the key qualifications someone needs to perform the job successfully.It spells out the important attributes of a person in terms of education, experience, skills, knowledge and abilities (SKAs) to perform a particular job. The job specification is a logical outgrowth of a job description. For each job description, it is desirable to have a job specification. This helps the organization to find what kinds of persons are needed to take up specific jobs.

Contents: A job specification usually covers the following information:

- Education
- Experience
- Skill, Knowledge, Abilities
- Work Orientation Factors
- Age

3.9.3. Selection Process

Selecting a suitable candidate can be the biggest challenge for any organization. The success of an organization largely depends on its staff. Selection of the right candidate builds the foundation of any organization's success and helps in reducing turnovers. Though there is no fool proof selection procedure that will ensure low turnover and high profits, the following steps generally make up the selection process-

a) Initial Screening

This is generally the starting point of any employee selection process. Initial Screening eliminates unqualified applicants and helps save time. Applications received from various sources are scrutinized and irrelevant ones are discarded.

b) Preliminary Interview

It is used to eliminate those candidates who do not meet the minimum eligibility criteria laid down by the organization. The skills, academic and family background, competencies and interests of the candidate are examined during preliminary interview. Preliminary interviews are less formalized and planned than the final interviews. The candidates are given a brief up about the company and the job profile; and it is also examined how much the candidate knows about the company. Preliminary interviews are also called screening interviews.

c) Filling Application Form

An candidate who passes the preliminary interview and is found to be eligible for the job is asked to fill in a formal application form. Such a form is designed in a way that it records the personal as well professional details of the candidates such as age, qualifications, reason for leaving previous job, experience, etc.

d) *Personal Interview*

Most employers believe that the personal interview is very important. It helps them in obtaining more information about the prospective employee. It also helps them in interacting with the candidate and judging his communication abilities, his ease of handling pressure etc. In some Companies, the selection process comprises only of the Interview.

e) *References Check*

Most application forms include a section that requires prospective candidates to put down names of a few references. References can be classified into - former employer, former customers, business references, reputable persons. Such references are contacted to get a feedback on the person in question including his behavior, skills, conduct etc.

f) *Background Verification*

A background check is a review of a person's commercial, criminal and (occasionally) financial records. Employers often perform background checks on employers or candidates for employment to confirm information given in a job application, verify a person's identity, or ensure that the individual does not have a history of criminal activity, etc., that could be an issue upon   employment.

g) *Final Interview*

Final interview is a process in which a potential employee is evaluated by an employer for prospective employment in their organization. During this process, the employer hopes to determine whether or not the applicant is suitable for the job. Different types of tests are conducted to evaluate the capabilities of an applicant, his behavior, special qualities etc. Separate tests are conducted for various types of jobs.

h) *Physical Examination*

If all goes well, then at this stage, a physical examination is conducted to make sure that the candidate has sound health and does not suffer from any serious ailment.

i) *Job Offer*

A candidate who clears all the steps is finally considered right for a particular job and is presented with the job offer. An applicant can be dropped at any given stage if considered unfit for the job.

3.10. Employee Induction /Orientation

Orientation or induction is the process of introducing new employees to an organization, to their specific jobs & departments, and in some instances, to their community.

Purposes of Orientation

Orientation isn't a nicety! It is used for the following purposes:

1. To Reduce Startup-Costs: Proper orientation can help the employee get "up to speed" much more quickly, thereby reducing the costs associated with learning the job.

2. To Reduce Anxiety: Any employee, when put into a new, strange situation, will experience anxiety that can impede his or her ability to learn to do the job. Proper orientation helps to reduce anxiety that results from entering into an unknown situation, and helps provide guidelines for behaviour and conduct, so the employee doesn't have to experience the stress of guessing.

3. To Reduce Employee Turnover: Employee turnover increases as employees feel they are not valued, or are put in positions where they can't possibly do their jobs. Orientation shows that the organization values the employee, and helps provide tools necessary for succeeding in the job.

4. To Save Time for Supervisor &Co-Workers: Simply put, the better the initial orientation, the less likely supervisors and co-workers will have to spend time teaching the employee.

5. To Develop Realistic Job Expectations, Positive Attitudes and Job Satisfaction: It is important that employees learn early on what is expected of them, and what to expect from others, in addition to learning about the values and attitudes of the organization. While people can learn from experience, they will make many mistakes that are unnecessary and potentially damaging.

    An orientation program principally conveys 3 types of information, namely:

    a) General information about the daily work routine to be followed

    b) A review of the organization's history, founders, objectives, operations & products or services, as well as how the employee's job contributes to the organization's needs.

    c) A detailed presentation of the organization's policies, work rules & employee benefits.

Two Kinds of Orientation

There are two related kinds of orientation. The first we will call Overview Orientation, and deals with the basic information an employee will need to understand the broader system he or she works in. Overview Orientation includes helping employees understand:

- Management in general
- Department and the branch
- Important policies
- General procedures (non-job specific)
- Information about compensation
- Accident prevention measures
- Employee and union issues (rights, responsibilities)
- Physical facilities

Often, Overview Orientation can be conducted by the personnel department with a little help from the branch manager or immediate supervisor, since much of the content is generic in nature.

The second kind of orientation is called Job-Specific Orientation, and is the process that is used to help employees understand:

- Function of the organization
- Responsibilities
- Expectations
- Duties
- Policies, procedures, rules and regulations
- Layout of workplace
- Introduction to co-workers and other people in the broader organization.

Job specific orientation is best conducted by the immediate supervisor, and/or manager, since much of the content will be specific to the individual. Often the orientation process will be ongoing, with supervisors and co-workers supplying coaching.

3.11. Career Development

Career development not only improves job performance but also brings about the growth of the personality. Individuals not only mature regarding their potential capacities but also become better individuals. Purpose of development Management development attempts to improve managerial performance by imparting.

- Knowledge
- Changing attitudes
- Increasing skills

The major objective of development is managerial effectiveness through a planned and a deliberate process of learning. This provides for a planned growth of managers to meet the future organizational needs.

Development Process

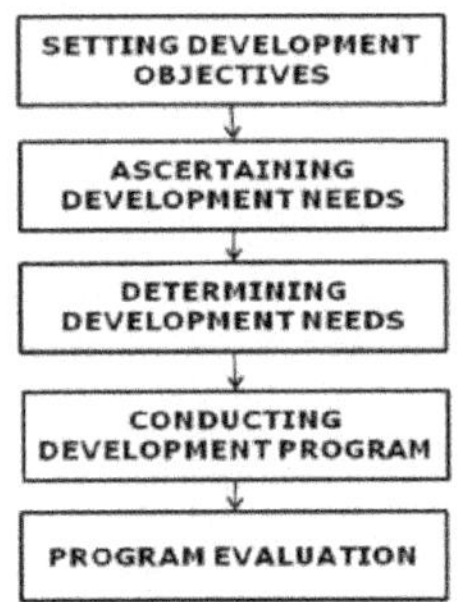

Fig 3.3: Development Process

The above diagram mention the development process, It consists of the following steps

1. **Setting Development Objectives:** It develops a framework from which executive need can be determined.
2. **Ascertaining Development Needs:** It aims at organizational planning & forecast the present and future growth.
3. **Determining Development Needs:** This consists of
   - Appraisal of present management talent
   - Management Manpower Inventory

   The above two processes will determine the skill deficiencies that are relative to the future needs of the organization.
4. **Conducting Development Programs:** It is carried out on the basis of needs of different individuals, differences in their attitudes and behavior, also their physical, intellectual and emotional qualities. Thus a comprehensive and well conceived program is prepared depending on the organizational needs and the time & cost involved.
5. **Program Evaluation:** It is an attempt to assess the value of training in order to achieve organizational objectives.

3.12. Training

Training is a process of learning a sequence of programmed behaviour. It improves the employee's performance on the current job and prepares them for an intended job.

Purpose of Training

1) To improve Productivity: Training leads to increased operational productivity and increased company profit.

2) To improve Quality:Better trained workers are less likely to make operational mistakes.

3) To improve Organizational Climate:Training leads to improved production and product quality which enhances financial incentives. This in turn increases the overall morale of the

organization.

4) To increase Health and Safety: Proper training prevents industrial accidents.

5) Personal Growth: Training gives employees a wider awareness, an enlarged skill base and that leads to enhanced personal growth.

Steps in Training Process

1. Identifying Training needs: A training program is designed to assist in providing solutions for specific operational problems or to improve performance of a trainee.

   - Organizational determination and Analysis: Allocation of resources that relate to organizational goal.

   - Operational Analysis: Determination of a specific employee behaviour required for a particular task.

   - Man Analysis: Knowledge, attitude and skill one must possess for attainment of organizational objectives

2. Getting ready for the job: The trainer has to be prepared for the job. And also who needs to be trained - the newcomer or the existing employee or the supervisory staff.
   Preparation of the learner:

   - Putting the learner at ease

   - Stating the importance and ingredients of the job

   - Creating interest

   - Placing the learner as close to his normal working position

   - Familiarizing him with the equipment, materials and trade terms

3. Presentation of Operation and Knowledge: The trainer should clearly tell, show, illustrate and question in order to convey the new knowledge and operations. The trainee should be encouraged to ask questions in order to indicate that he really knows and understands the job.

4. Performance Try out: The trainee is asked to go through the job several times. This gradually builds up his skill, speed and confidence.

5. Follow-up: This evaluates the effectiveness of the entire training effort

3.12.1. Training Methods

Training methods can be broadly classified as on-the-job training and off-the-job training

a) On-the-job Training

On the job training occurs when workers pick up skills whilst working along side experienced workers at their place of work. For example this could be the actual assembly line or offices where the employee works. New workers may simply **"shadow"** or observe fellow employees to begin with and are often given instruction manuals or interactive training programmes to work through.

b) Off-the-job Training

This occurs when workers are taken away from their place of work to be trained. This may take place at training agency or local college, although many larger firms also have their own training centers. Training can take the form of lectures or self-study and can be used to develop more general skills and knowledge that can be used in a variety of situations.

The various types of off-the-job training are

i. Instructor presentation: The trainer orally presents new information to the trainees, usually through lecture. Instructor presentation may include classroom lecture, seminar, workshop, and the like.

ii. Group discussion: The trainer leads the group of trainees in discussing a topic.

iii. Demonstration: The trainer shows the correct steps for completing a task, or shows an example of a correctly completed task.

iv. Assigned reading: The trainer gives the trainees reading assignments that provide new information.

v. Exercise: The trainer assigns problems to be solved either on paper or in real situations related to the topic of the training activity.

vi.   Case study: The trainer gives the trainees information about a situation and directs them to come to a decision or solve a problem concerning the situation.

vii.   Role play: Trainees act out a real-life situation in an instructional setting.

viii.   Field visit and study tour: Trainees are given the opportunity to observe and interact with the problem being solved or skill being learned.

3.13. Career Stages

What people want from their careers also varies according to the stage of one's career. What may have been important in an early stage may not be important in a later one. Four distinct career stages have been identified: trial, establishment/advancement, mid-career, and late career. Each stage represents different career needs and interests of the individual

a) **Trial stage:** The trial stage begins with an individual's exploration of career-related matters and ends usually at about age 25 with a commitment on the part of the individual to a particular occupation. Until the decision is made to settle down, the individual may try a number of jobs and a number of organizations. Unfortunately for many organizations, this trial and exploration stage results in high level of turnover among new employees. Employees in this stage need opportunities for self-exploration and a variety of job activities or assignments.

b) **Establishment Stage:** The establishment/advancement stage tends to occur between ages 25 and 44. In this stage, the individual has made his or her career choice and is concerned with achievement, performance, and advancement. This stage is marked by high employee productivity and career growth, as the individual is motivated to succeed in the organization and in his or her chosen occupation. Opportunities for job challenge and use of special competencies are desired in this stage. The employee strives for creativity and innovation through new job assignments. Employees also need a certain degree of autonomy in this stage so that they can experience feelings of individual achievement and personal success.

c) **Mid Career Crisis Sub Stage:** The period occurring between the mid-thirties and mid-forties during which people often make a major reassessment of their progress relative to their original career ambitions and goals.

d) **Maintenance stage:** The mid-career stage, which occurs roughly between the ages 45 and 64, has also been referred to as the maintenance stage. This stage is typified by a continuation of established patterns of work behavior. The person is no longer trying to establish a place for himself or herself in the organization, but seeks to maintain his or her position. This stage is viewed as a mid-career plateau in which little new ground is broken. The individual in this stage may need some technical updating in his or her field. The employee should be encouraged to develop new job skills in order to avoid early stagnation and decline.

e) **Late-career stage:** In this stage the career lessens in importance and the employee plans for retirement and seeks to develop a sense of identity outside the work environment.

3.14. Performance Appraisal

Performance appraisal is the process of obtaining, analyzing and recording information about the relative worth of an employee. The focus of the performance appraisal is measuring and improving the actual performance of the employee and also the future potential of the employee. Its aim is to measure what an employee does.

3.14.1. Objectives of Performance Appraisal

- To review the performance of the employees over a given period of time.
- To judge the gap between the actual and the desired performance.
- To help the management in exercising organizational control.
- Helps to strengthen the relationship and communication between superior - subordinates and management - employees.
- To diagnose the strengths and weaknesses of the individuals so as to identify the training and development needs of the future.
- To provide feedback to the employees regarding their past performance.
- Provide information to assist in the other personal decisions in the organization.
- Provide clarity of the expectations and responsibilities of the functions to be performed by the employees.
- To judge the effectiveness of the other human resource functions of the organization such as recruitment, selection, training and development.
- To reduce the grievances of the employees.

The Process of performance appraisal is explained in the following Fig 3.4.

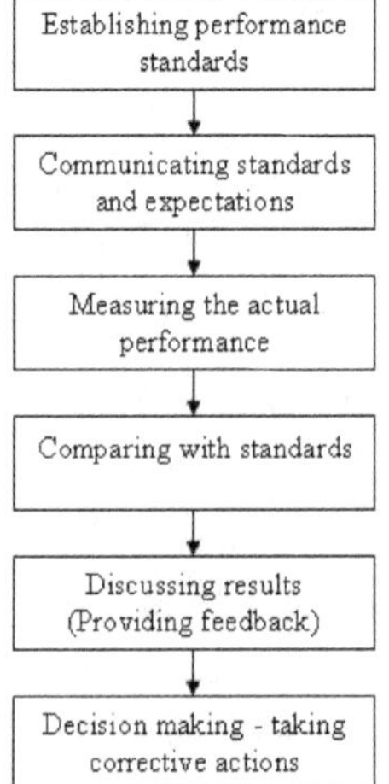

Fig 3.4: Process of Performance Appraisal

a) *Establishing Performance Standards*

The first step in the process of performance appraisal is the setting up of the standards which will be used to as the base to compare the actual performance of the employees. This step requires setting the criteria to judge the performance of the employees as successful or unsuccessful and the degrees of their contribution to the organizational goals and objectives. The standards set should be clear, easily understandable and in measurable terms. In case the performance of the employee cannot be measured, great care should be taken to describe the standards.

b) *Communicating the Standards*

After establishing the standards, it is the responsibility of the management to communicate the standards to all the employees of the organization. The employees should be informed and the standards should be clearly explained to them. This will help them to understand their roles and to know what exactly is expected from them. The standards should also be communicated to the appraisers or the evaluators and if required, the standards can also be modified at this stage itself according to the relevant feedback from the employees or the evaluators.

c) Measuring the Actual Performance

The most difficult part of the Performance appraisal process is measuring the actual performance of the employees that is the work done by the employees during the specified period of time. It is a continuous process which involves monitoring the performance throughout the year. This stage requires the careful selection of the appropriate techniques of measurement, taking care that personal bias does not affect the outcome of the process and providing assistance rather than interfering in an employees work.

d) Comparing the Actual with the Desired Performance

The actual performance is compared with the desired or the standard performance. The comparison tells the deviations in the performance of the employees from the standards set. The result can show the actual performance being more than the desired performance or, the actual performance being less than the desired performance depicting a negative deviation in the organizational performance. It includes recalling, evaluating and analysis of data related to the employees' performance.

e) Discussing Results

The result of the appraisal is communicated and discussed with the employees on one-to-one basis. The focus of this discussion is on communication and listening. The results, the problems and the possible solutions are discussed with the aim of problem solving and reaching consensus. The feedback should be given with a positive attitude as this can have an effect on the employees' future performance. The purpose of the meeting should be to solve the problems faced and motivate the employees to perform better.

f) Decision Making

The last step of the process is to take decisions which can be taken either to improve the performance of the employees, take the required corrective actions, or the related HR decisions like rewards, promotions, demotions, transfers etc.

Unit IV

Directing

4.1. Definition

"Activating deals with the steps a manager takes to get sub-ordinates and others to carry out plans" - Newman and Warren. Directing concerns the total manner in which a manager influences the actions of subordinates. It is the final action of a manager in getting others to act after all preparations have been completed.

Characteristics

- Elements of Management
- Continuing Function
- Pervasive Function
- Creative Function
- Linking function
- Management of Human Factor

Scope of Directing

- Initiates action
- Ensures coordination
- Improves efficiency
- Facilitates change
- Assists stability and growth

4.1.1. Elements of Directing

The three elements of directing are

- Motivation
- Leadership
- Communication

4.2. Creativity and Innovation

Often used interchangeably, they should to be considered separate and distinct. Creativity can be described as problem identification and idea generation and innovation is considered as idea selection, development and commercialization. Creativity is creation of new ideas and Innovation is implementation of the new ideas. There cannot be innovation without creativity. There can be creativity without innovation but it has no value.

The various Steps involved in the creativity is explained in the following Fig 4.1.

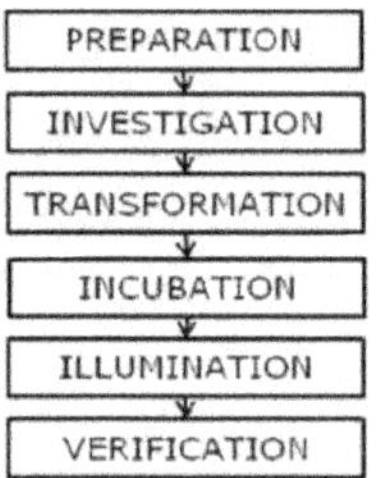

Fig 4.1: Creativity

a. **Preparation:** This is the first stage at which the base for creativity and innovation is defined; the mind is prepared for subsequent use in creative thinking. During preparation the individual is encouraged to appreciate the fact that every opportunity provides situations that can educate and experiences from which to learn. The creativity aspect is kindled through a quest to become more knowledgeable. This can be done through reading about various topics and/or subjects and engaging in discussions with others. Taking part in brainstorming sessions in various forums like professional and trade association seminars, and taking time to study other countries and cultures to identify viable opportunities is also part of preparation. Of importance is the need to cultivate a personal ability to listen and learn from others.

b. **Investigation:** This stage of enhancing entrepreneurial creativity and innovation involves the business owner taking time to study the problem at hand and what its various components are.

c. **Transformation:** The information thus accumulated and acquired should then be subjected to convergent and divergent thinking which will serve to highlight the inherent similarities and differences. Convergent thinking will help identify aspects that are similar and connected while divergent thinking will highlight the differences.

This twin manner of thinking is of particular importance in realizing creativity and innovation for the following reasons:

- One will be able to skim the details and see what the bigger picture is the situation/problem's components can be reordered and in doing so new patterns can be identified.
- It will help visualize a number of approaches that can be used to simultaneously tackle the problem and the opportunity.
- One's decision-making abilities will be bettered such that the urge to make snap decisions will be resisted.

d. **Incubation:** At this stage in the quest for creativity and innovation it is imperative that the subconscious reflect on the accumulated information, i.e. through incubation, and this can be improved or augmented when the entrepreneur:

- Engages in an activity completely unrelated to the problem/opportunity under scrutiny.
- Takes time to daydream i.e. letting the mind roam beyond any restrictions self-imposed or otherwise.
- Relax and play
- Study the problem/opportunity in a wholly different environment

e. **Illumination:** This happens during the incubation stage and will often be spontaneous. The realizations from the past stages combine at this instance to form a breakthrough.

f. **Verification:** This is where the entrepreneur attempts to ascertain whether the creativity of thought and the action of innovation are truly effective as anticipated. It may involve activities like simulation, piloting, prototype building, test marketing, and various experiments. While the tendency to ignore this stage and plunge headlong with the breakthrough may be tempting, the transformation stage should ensure that the new idea is put to the test.

4.3. Motivation and Satisfaction

Motivation

"Motivation" is a Latin word, meaning "to move". Human motives are internalized goals within individuals. Motivation may be defined as those forces that cause people to behave in certain ways. Motivation encompasses all those pressures and influences that trigger, channel, and sustain human behavior. Most successful managers have learned to understand the concept of human motivation and are able to use that understanding to achieve higher standards of subordinate work performance.

According to Koontz and O'Donnell, "Motivation is a class of drives, needs, wishes and similar forces".

4.3.1. *Nature and Characteristics of Motivation*

Psychologists generally agree that all behavior is motivated, and that people have reasons for doing the things they do or for behaving in the manner that they do. Motivating is the work a manager performs to inspire, encourage and impel people to take required action.

The characteristics of motivation are given below:-

Motivation is an Internal Feeling

Motivation is a psychological phenomenon which generates in the mind of an individual the feeling that he lacks certain things and needs those things. Motivation is a force within an individual that drives him to behave in a certain way.

Motivation is Related to Needs

Needs are deficiencies which are created whenever there is a physiological or psychological imbalance. In order to motivate a person, we have to understand his needs that call for satisfaction.

Motivation Produces Goal-Directed behaviour

Goals are anything which will alleviate a need and reduce a drive. An individual's behavior is directed towards a goal.

Motivation can be Either Positive or Negative

Positive or incentive motivation is generally based on reward. According to Flippo - "positive motivation is a process of attempting to influence others to do your will through the possibility of gain or reward".

4.3.2. *Importance of Motivation*

A manager's primary task is to motivate others to perform the tasks of the organization. Therefore, the manager must find the keys to get subordinates to come to work regularly and on time, to work hard, and to make positive contributions towards the effective and efficient achievement of organizational objectives. Motivation is an effective instrument in the hands of a manager for inspiring the work force and creating confidence in it. By motivating the work force, management creates "will to work" which is necessary for the achievement of organizational goals. The various benefits of motivation are:

- Motivation is one of the important elements in the directing process. By motivating the workers, a manager directs or guides the workers' actions in the desired direction for accomplishing the goals of the organization.

- Workers will tend to be as efficient as possible by improving upon their skills and knowledge so that they are able to contribute to the progress of the organization thereby increasing productivity.

- For performing any tasks, two things are necessary. They are: (a) ability to work and (b) willingness to work. Without willingness to work, ability to work is of no use. The willingness to work can be created only by motivation.

- Organizational effectiveness becomes, to some degree, a question of management's ability to motivate its employees, to direct at least a reasonable effort towards the goals of the organization.

- Motivation contributes to good industrial relations in the organization. When the workers are motivated, contented and disciplined, the frictions between the workers and the management will be reduced.

- Motivation is the best remedy for resistance to changes. When changes are introduced in an organization, generally, there will be resistance from the workers. But if the workers of an organization are motivated, they will accept, introduce and implement the changes whole heartily and help to keep the organization on the right track of progress.

- Motivation facilitates the maximum utilization of all factors of production, human, physical and financial resources and thereby contributes to higher production.

- Motivation promotes a sense of belonging among the workers. The workers feel that the enterprise belongs to them and the interest of the enterprise is their interests.

- Many organizations are now beginning to pay increasing attention to developing their employees as future resources upon which they can draw as they grow and develop.

4.4. Satisfaction

Employee satisfaction (Job satisfaction) is the terminology used to describe whether employees are happy and contented and fulfilling their desires and needs at work. Many measures purport that employee satisfaction is a factor in employee motivation, employee goal achievement, and positive employee morale in the workplace.

Employee satisfaction, while generally a positive in your organization, can also be a downer if mediocre employees stay because they are satisfied with your work environment. Factors contributing to employee satisfaction include treating employees with respect,providing regular employee recognition, empowering employees, offering above industry-average benefits and compensation, providing employee perks and company activities, and positive management within a success framework of goals, measurements, and expectations.

Employee satisfaction is often measured by anonymous employee satisfaction surveys administered periodically that gauge employee satisfaction in areas such as:

- management
- understanding of mission and vision
- empowerment
- teamwork
- communication, and
- Coworker interaction

The facets of employee satisfaction measured vary from company to company.

A second method used to measure employee satisfaction is meeting with small groups of employees and asking the same questions verbally. Depending on the culture of the company, either method can contribute knowledge about employee satisfaction to managers and employees.

4.5. Job Design

It is the process of Work arrangement (or rearrangement)aimed at reducing or overcoming job dissatisfaction and employee alienation arising from repetitive and mechanistic tasks. Through job design, organizations try to raise productivity levels by offering non-monetary rewards such as greater satisfaction from a sense of personal achievement in meeting the increased challenge and responsibility of one's work.

Approaches to Job Design Include

Job Enlargement

Job enlargement changes the jobs to include more and/or different tasks. Job enlargement should add interest to the work but may or may not give employees more responsibility.

Job Rotation

Job rotation moves employees from one task to another. It distributes the group tasks among a number of employees.

Job Enrichment

Job enrichment allows employees to assume more responsibility, accountability, and independence when learning new tasks or to allow for greater participation and new opportunities.

4.6.   Types of Motivation Techniques

If a manager wants to get work done by his employees, he may either hold out a promise of a reward (positive motivation) or he/she may install fear (negative motivation). Both these types are widely used by managements.

a) Positive Motivation

This type of motivation is generally based on reward. A positive motivation involves the possibility of increased motive satisfaction. According to Flippo-"Positive motivation is a process of attempting to influence others to do your will through the possibility of gain or reward". Incentive motivation is the "pull" mechanism. The receipt of awards, due recognition and praise for work-well done definitely lead to good team spirit, co-operation and a feeling of happiness.

Positive motivation include:

- Praise and credit for work done
- Wages and Salaries
- Appreciation
- A sincere interest in subordinates as individuals
- Delegation of authority and responsibility

b) Negative Motivation

This type of motivation is based on force and fear. Fear causes persons to act in a certain way because they fear the consequences. Negative motivation involves the possibility of decreased motive satisfaction. It is a "push" mechanism. The imposition of punishment frequently results in frustration among those punished, leading to the development of maladaptive behaviour. It also creates a hostile state of mind and an unfavourable attitude to the job. However, there is no management which has not used the negative motivation at some time or the other.

4.7.   Motivation Theories

Some of the motivation theories are discussed below

a) McGregor's Theory X and Theory Y

McGregor states that people inside the organization can be managed in two ways. The first is basically negative, which falls under the category X and the other is basically positive, which falls under the category Y. After viewing the way in which the manager dealt with employees, McGregor concluded that a manager's view of the nature of human beings is based on a certain grouping of assumptions and that he or she tends to mold his or her behavior towards subordinates according to these assumptions.

Under the Assumptions of Theory X

- Employees inherently do not like work and whenever possible, will attempt to avoid it.
- Because employees dislike work, they have to be forced, coerced or threatened with punishment to achieve goals.
- Employees avoid responsibilities and do not work fill formal directions are issued.
- Most workers place a greater importance on security over all other factors and display little ambition.

Under the Assumptions of Theory Y

- Physical and mental effort at work is as natural as rest or play.
- People do exercise self-control and self-direction and if they are committed to those goals.
- Average human beings are willing to take responsibility and exercise imagination, ingenuity and creativity in solving the problems of the organization.
- That the way the things are organized, the average human being's brainpower is only partly used.

On analysis of the assumptions it can be detected that theory X assumes that lower-order needs dominate individuals and theory Y assumes that higher-order needs dominate individuals. An organization that is run on Theory X lines tends to be authoritarian in nature, the word "authoritarian" suggests such ideas as the "power to enforce obedience" and the "right to command." In contrast Theory Y organizations can be described as "participative", where the aims of the organization and of the individuals in it are integrated; individuals can achieve their own goals best by directing their efforts towards the success of the organization.

b) *Abraham Maslow's "Need Hierarchy Theory"*

One of the most widely mentioned theories of motivation is the hierarchy of needs theory put forth by psychologist Abraham Maslow. Maslow saw human needs in the form of a hierarchy, ascending from the lowest to the highest, and he concluded that when one set of needs is satisfied, this kind of need ceases to be a motivator. As per his theory these needs are:

i. *Physiological Needs*

These are important needs for sustaining the human life. Food, water, warmth, shelter, sleep, medicine and education are the basic physiological needs which fall in the primary list of need satisfaction. Maslow was of an opinion that until these needs were satisfied to a degree to maintain life, no other motivating factors can work.

ii. *Security or Safety Needs*

These are the needs to be free of physical danger and of the fear of losing a job, property, food or shelter. It also includes protection against any emotional harm.

iii. *Social Needs*

Since people are social beings, they need to belong and be accepted by others. People try to satisfy their need for affection, acceptance and friendship.

iv. *Esteem needs*

According to Maslow, once people begin to satisfy their need to belong, they tend to want to be held in esteem both by themselves and by others. This kind of need produces such satisfaction as power, prestige status and self-confidence. It includes both internal esteem factors like self-respect, autonomy and achievements and external esteem factors such as states, recognition and attention.

v. *Need for Self-actualization*

Maslow regards this as the highest need in his hierarchy. It is the drive to become what one is capable of becoming; it includes growth, achieving one's potential and self-fulfillment. It is to maximize one's potential and to accomplish something.

All of the needs are structured into a hierarchy and only once a lower level of need has been fully met, would a worker be motivated by the opportunity of having the next need up in the hierarchy satisfied. For example a person who is dying of hunger will be motivated to achieve a basic wage in order to buy food before worrying about having a secure job contract or the respect of others.

A business should therefore offer different incentives to workers in order to help them fulfill each need in turn and progress up the hierarchy. Managers should also recognize that workers are not all motivated in the same way and do not all move up the hierarchy at the same pace. They may therefore have to offer a slightly different set of incentives from worker to worker.

c) *Frederick Herzberg's Motivation-Hygiene Theory*

Frederick has tried to modify Maslow's need Hierarchy theory. His theory is also known as two-factor theory or Hygiene theory. He stated that there are certain satisfiers and dissatisfies for employees at work. Intrinsic factors are related to job satisfaction, while extrinsic factors are associated with dissatisfaction. He devised his theory on the question: "What do people want from their jobs?" He asked people to describe in detail, such situations when they felt exceptionally good or exceptionally bad. From the responses that he received, he concluded that opposite of satisfaction is not dissatisfaction. Removing dissatisfying characteristics from a job does not necessarily make the job satisfying. He states that presence of certain factors in the organization is natural and the presence of the same does not lead to motivation. However, their non-presence leads to de-motivation. In similar manner there are certain factors, the absence of which causes no dissatisfaction, but their presence has motivational impact. Examples of Hygiene factors are: Security, status, relationship with subordinates, personal life, salary, work conditions, relationship with supervisor and company policy and administration.Examples of Motivational factors are: Growth prospectus job advancement, responsibility, challenges, recognition and achievements.

d) *Victor Vroom's Expectancy Theory*

The most widely accepted explanations of motivation have been propounded by Victor Vroom. His theory is commonly known as expectancy theory. The theory argues that the strength of a tendency to act in a specific way depends on the strength of an expectation that the act will be followed by a given outcome and on the attractiveness of that outcome to the individual to make this simple, expectancy theory says that an employee can be motivated to perform better when there is a belief that the better performance will lead to good performance appraisal and that this shall result into realization of personal goal in form of some reward. Therefore an employee is: Motivation = Valence x Expectancy. The theory focuses on three things:

- Efforts and performance relationship
- Performance and reward relationship
- Rewards and personal goal relationship

e) *Clayton Alderfer's ERG Theory*

Alderfer has tried to rebuild the hierarchy of needs of Maslow into another model named ERG i.e. Existence - Relatedness - Growth. According to him there are 3 groups of core needs as mentioned above. The existence group is concerned mainly with providing basic material existence. The second group is the individuals need to maintain interpersonal relationship with other members in the group. The final group is the intrinsic desire to grow and develop personally.

The major conclusions of this theory are

- In an individual, more than one need may be operative at the same time.
- If a higher need goes unsatisfied than the desire to satisfy a lower need intensifies.
- It also contains the frustration-regression dimension.

f) *McClelland's Theory of Needs*

David McClelland has developed a theory on three types of motivating needs:

i. Need for Power
ii. Need for Affiliation
iii. Need for Achievement

Basically people for high need for power are inclined towards influence and control. They like to be at the center and are good orators.They are demanding in nature, forceful in manners and ambitious in life. They can be motivated to perform if they are given key positions or power positions.

In the second category are the people who are social in nature. They try to affiliate themselves with individuals and groups. They are driven by love and faith. They like to build a friendly environment around themselves. Social recognition and affiliation with others provides them motivation.

People in the third area are driven by the challenge of success and the fear of failure. Their need for achievement is moderate and they set for themselves moderately difficult tasks. They are analytical in nature and take calculated risks. Such people are motivated to perform when they see at least some chances of success.

McClelland observed that with the advancement in hierarchy the need for power and achievement increased rather than Affiliation. He also observed that people who were at the top, later ceased to be motivated by this drives.

g) *Stacey Adams' Equity Theory*

As per the equity theory of J. Stacey Adams, people are motivated by their beliefs about the reward structure as being fair or unfair, relative to the inputs. People have a tendency to use subjective judgment to balance the outcomes and inputs in the relationship for comparisons between different individuals. If people feel that they are not equally rewarded they either reduce the quantity or quality of work or migrate to some other organization. However, if people perceive that they are rewarded higher, they may be motivated to work harder.

h) *Skinner's Reinforcement Theory*

B.F. Skinner, who propounded the reinforcement theory, holds that by designing the environment properly, individuals can be motivated. Instead of considering internal factors like impressions, feelings, attitudes and other cognitive behavior, individuals are directed by what happens in the environment external to them. Skinner states that work environment should be made suitable to the individuals and that punishment actually leads to frustration and demotivation. Hence, the only way to motivate is to keep on making positive changes in the external environment of the organization.

4.8. Leadership

Definition

Leadership is defined as influence, the art or process of influencing people so that they will strive willingly and enthusiastically toward the achievement of group goals.

- Leaders act to help a group attain objectives through the maximum application of its capabilities.
- Leaders must instill values - whether it be concern for quality, honesty and calculated risk taking or for employees and customers.

4.8.1. *Importance of Leadership*

1. Aid to authority
2. Motive power to group efforts
3. Basis for co operation
4. Integration of Formal and Informal Organization.

4.8.2. *Leadership Styles*

The leadership style we will discuss here are:

a) Autocratic style

b) Democratic Style

c) Laissez Faire Style

a) *Autocratic Style*

Manager retains as much power and decision-making authority as possible. The manager does not consult employees, nor are they allowed to give any input. Employees are expected to obey orders without receiving any explanations. The motivation environment is produced by creating a structured set of rewards and punishments.

Autocratic leadership is a classical leadership style with the following characteristics:

- Manager seeks to make as many decisions as possible
- Manager seeks to have the most authority and control in decision making
- Manager seeks to retain responsibility rather than utilize complete delegation
- Consultation with other colleagues in minimal and decision making becomes a solitary process
- Managers are less concerned with investing their own leadership development, and prefer to simply work on the task at hand.

Advantages

- Reduced stress due to increased control
- A more productive group 'while the leader is watching'
- Improved logistics of operations
- Faster decision making

Disadvantages

- Manager perceived as having poor leadership skills
- Increased workload for the manager
- People dislike being ordered around
- Teams become dependent upon their leader

b) *Democratic Style*

Democratic Leadership is the leadership style that promotes the sharing of responsibility, the exercise of delegation and continual consultation.

The Style has the following Characteristics

- Manager seeks consultation on all major issues and decisions.
- Manager effectively delegate tasks to subordinates and give them full control and responsibility for those tasks.
- Manager welcomes feedback on the results of initiatives and the work environment.
- Manager encourages others to become leaders and be involved in leadership development.

Advantages

- Positive work environment Successful initiatives
- Creative thinking
- Reduction of friction and office politics
- Reduced employee turnover

Disadvantages

- Takes long time to take decisions
- Danger of pseudo participation
- Like the other styles, the democratic style is not always appropriate.
- It is most successful when used with highly skilled or experienced employees or when implementing operational changes or resolving individual or group problems.

c) *Laissez-Faire Style*

This French phrase means "leave it be" and is used to describe a leader who leaves his/her colleagues to get on with their work. The style is largely a "hands off" view that tends to minimize the amount of direction and face time required.

Advantages

- No work for the leader
- Frustration may force others into leadership roles
- Allows the visionary worker the opportunity to do what they want, free from interference
- Empowers the group

Disadvantages

- It makes employees feel insecure at the unavailability of a manager.
- The manager cannot provide regular feedback to let employees know how well they are doing.
- Managers are unable to thank employees for their good work.
- The manager doesn't understand his or her responsibilities and is hoping the employees can cover for him or her.

4.8.3. Leadership Theories

The various leadership theories are

a) Great Man Theory

Assumptions

- Leaders are born and not made.
- Great leaders will arise when there is a great need.

Description

Early research on leadership was based on the study of people who were already great leaders. These people were often from the aristocracy, as few from lower classes had the opportunity to lead. This contributed to the notion that leadership had something to do with breeding. The idea of the Great Man also strayed into the mythic domain, with notions that in times of need, a Great Man would arise, almost by magic. This was easy to verify, by pointing to people such as Eisenhower and Churchill, let alone those further back along the timeline, even to Jesus, Moses, Mohammed and the Buddah.

Discussion

Gender issues were not on the table when the 'Great Man' theory was proposed. Most leaders were male and the thought of a Great Woman was generally in areas other than leadership. Most researchers were also male, and concerns about andocentric bias were a long way from being realized.

b) Trait Theory

Assumptions

- People are born with inherited traits.
- Some traits are particularly suited to leadership.
- People who make good leaders have the right (or sufficient) combination of traits.

Description

Early research on leadership was based on the psychological focus of the day, which was of people having inherited characteristics or traits. Attention was thus put on discovering these traits, often by studying successful leaders, but with the underlying assumption that if other people could also be found with these traits, then they, too, could also become great leaders.

McCall and Lombardo (1983) researched both success and failure identified four primary traits by which leaders could succeed or 'derail': Emotional stability and composure: Calm, confident and predictable, particularly when under stress.

Admitting error: Owning up to mistakes, rather than putting energy into covering up.

Good interpersonal skills: able to communicate and persuade others without resort to negative or coercive tactics.

Intellectual breadth: Able to understand a wide range of areas, rather than having a narrow (and narrow-minded) area of expertise.

c) Behavioral Theory

Assumptions

- Leaders can be made, rather than are born.
- Successful leadership is based in definable, learnable behavior.

Description

Behavioral theories of leadership do not seek inborn traits or capabilities. Rather, they look at what leaders actually do. If success can be defined in terms of describable actions, then it should be relatively easy for other people to act in the same way. This is easier to teach and learn then to adopt the more ephemeral 'traits' or 'capabilities'.

d) Participative Leadership

Assumptions

- Involvement in decision-making improves the understanding of the issues involved by those who must carry out the decisions.
- People are more committed to actions where they have involved in the relevant decisionmaking.
- People are less competitive and more collaborative when they are working on joint goals.

- When people make decisions together, the social commitment to one another is greater and thus increases their commitment to the decision.
- Several people deciding together make better decisions than one person alone.

Description

A Participative Leader, rather than taking autocratic decisions, seeks to involve other people in the process, possibly including subordinates, peers, superiors and other stake holders. Often, however, as it is within the managers' whim to give or deny control to his or her subordinates, most participative activity is within the immediate team. The question of how much influence others are given thus may vary on the manager's preferences and beliefs, and a whole spectrum of participation is possible

e) Situational Leadership

Assumptions

- The best action of the leader depends on a range of situational factors.

Description

When a decision is needed, an effective leader does not just fall into a single preferred style. In practice, as they say, things are not that simple. Factors that affect situational decisions include motivation and capability of followers. This, in turn, is affected by factors within the particular situation. The relationship between followers and the leader may be another factor that affects leader behavior as much as it does follower behavior.

The leaders' perception of the follower and the situation will affect what they do rather than the truth of the situation. The leader's perception of themselves and other factors such as stress and mood will also modify the leaders' behavior.

f) Contingency Theory

Assumptions

- The leader's ability to lead is contingent upon various situational factors, including the leader's preferred style, the capabilities and behaviors of followers and also various other situational factors.

Description

Contingency theories are a class of behavioral theory that contend that there is no one best way of leading and that a leadership style that is effective in some situations may not be successful in others. An effect of this is that leaders who are very effective at one place and time may become unsuccessful either when transplanted to another situation or when the factors around them change.

Contingency theory is similar to situational theory in that there is an assumption of no simple one right way. The main difference is that situational theory tends to focus more on the behaviors that the leader should adopt, given situational factors (often about follower behavior), whereas contingency theory takes a broader view that includes contingent factors about leader capability and other variables within the situation.

g) *Transactional Leadership*

Assumptions

- People are motivated by reward and punishment.
- Social systems work best with a clear chain of command.
- When people have agreed to do a job, a part of the deal is that they cede all authority to their manager.
- The prime purpose of a subordinate is to do what their manager tells them to do.

Description

The transactional leader works through creating clear structures whereby it is clear what is required of their subordinates, and the rewards that they get for following orders. Punishments are not always mentioned, but they are also well-understood and formal systems of discipline are usually in place.

The early stage of Transactional Leadership is in negotiating the contract whereby the subordinate is given a salary and other benefits, and the company (and by implication the subordinate's manager) gets authority over the subordinate.

When the Transactional Leader allocates work to a subordinate, they are considered to be fully responsible for it, whether or not they have the resources or capability to carry it out. When things go wrong, then the subordinate is considered to be personally at fault, and is punished for their failure (just as they are rewarded for succeeding).

h) *Transformational Leadership*

Assumptions

- People will follow a person who inspires them.
- A person with vision and passion can achieve great things.
- The way to get things done is by injecting enthusiasm and energy.

Description

Working for a Transformational Leader can be a wonderful and uplifting experience. They put passion and energy into everything. They care about you and want you to succeed.

Transformational Leaders are often charismatic, but are not as narcissistic as pure Charismatic Leaders, who succeed through a belief in themselves rather than a belief in others. One of the traps of Transformational Leadership s that passion and confidence can easily be mistaken for truth and reality.

Transformational Leaders, by definition, seek to transform. When the organization does not need transforming and people are happy as they are, then such a leader will be frustrated. Like wartime leaders, however, given the right situation they come into their own and can be personally responsible for saving entire companies.

4.9. Communication

Communication is the exchange of messages between people for the purpose of achieving common meanings. Unless common meanings are shared, managers find it extremely difficult to influence others. Whenever group of people interact, communication takes place. Communication is the exchange of information using a shared set of symbols. It is the process that links group members and enables them to coordinate their activities. Therefore, when managers foster effective communication, they strengthen the connections between employees and build cooperation. Communication also functions to build and reinforce interdependence between various parts of the organization. As a linking mechanism among the different organizational subsystems, communication is a central feature of the structure of groups and organizations. It helps to coordinate tasks and activities within and between organizations.

Definition

According to Koontz and O'Donnell, "Communication, is an intercourse by words, letters symbols or messages, and is a way that the organization members shares meaning and understanding with another".

4.9.1. The Communication Process

Communication is important in building and sustaining human relationships at work. Communication can be thought of as a process or flow. Before communication can take place, a purpose, expressed as a message to be conveyed is needed. It passes between the sender and the receiver. The result is transference of meaning from one person to another. The figure 4.2. below depicts the communication process. This model is made up of seven parts: (1) Source, (2) Encoding, (3) Message, (4) Channel, (5) Decoding, (6) Receiver, and (7) Feedback.

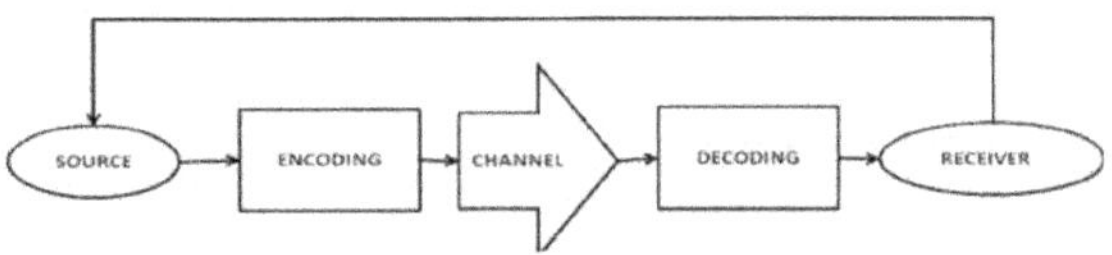

Fig 4.2: Communication Process

a) Source

The source initiates a message. This is the origin of the communication and can be an individual, group or inanimate object. The effectiveness of a communication depends to a considerable degree on the characteristics of the source. The person who initiates the communication process is known as sender, source or communicator. In an organization, the sender will be a person who has a need or desire to send a message to others. The sender has some information which he wants to communicate to some other person to achieve some purpose. By initiating the message, the sender attempts to achieve understanding and change in the behaviour of the receiver.

b) Encoding

Once the source has decided what message to communicate, the content of the message must be put in a form the receiver can understand. As the background for encoding information, the sender uses his or her own frame of reference. It includes the individual's view of the organization or situation as a function of personal education, interpersonal relationships, attitudes, knowledge and experience. Three conditions are necessary for successful encoding the message.

- Skill: Successful communicating depends on the skill you posses. Without the requisite skills, the message of the communicator will not reach the requisite skills; the message of the communicator will not reach the receiver in the desired form. One's total communicative success includes speaking, reading, listening and reasoning skills.

- Attitudes: Our attitudes influence our behaviour. We hold predisposed ideas on a number of topics and our communications are affected by these attitudes.

- Knowledge: We cannot communicate what we don't know. The amount of knowledge the source holds about his or her subject will affect the message he or she seeks to transfer.

c) The Message

The message is the actual physical product from the source encoding. The message contains the thoughts and feelings that the communicator intends to evoke in the receiver. The message has two primary components:-

- The Content: The thought or conceptual component of the message is contained in the words, ideas, symbols and concepts chosen to relay the message.

- The Affect: The feeling or emotional component of the message is contained in the intensity, force, demeanour (conduct or behaviour), and sometimes the gestures of the communicator.

d) The Channel

The actual means by which the message is transmitted to the receiver (Visual, auditory, written or some combination of these three) is called the channel. The channel is the medium through which the message travels. The channel is the observable carrier of the message. Communication in which the sender's voice is used as the channel is called oral communication. When the channel involves written language, the sender is using written communication. The sender's choice of a channel conveys additional information beyond that contained in the message itself. For example, documenting an employee's poor performance in writing conveys that the manager has taken the problem seriously.

e) Decoding

Decoding means interpreting what the message means. The extent to which the decoding by the receiver depends heavily on the individual characteristics of the sender and receiver. The greater the similarity in the background or status factors of the communicators, the greater the probability that a message will be perceived accurately. Most messages can be decoded in more than one way. Receiving and decoding a message are a type of perception. The decoding process is therefore subject to the perception biases.

f)   The Receiver

The receiver is the object to whom the message is directed. Receiving the message means one or more of the receiver's senses register the message-for example, hearing the sound of a supplier's voice over the telephone or seeing the boss give a thumbs-up signal. Like the sender, the receiver is subject to many influences that can affect the understanding of the message. Most important, the receiver will perceive a communication in a manner that is consistent with previous experiences. Communications that are not consistent with expectations is likely to be rejected.

g)   Feedback

The final link in the communication process is a feedback loop. Feedback, in effect, is communication travelling in the opposite direction. If the sender pays attention to the feedback and interprets it accurately, the feedback can help the sender learn whether the original communication was decoded accurately. Without feedback, one-way communication occurs between managers and their employees. Faced with differences in their power, lack of time, and a desire to save face by not passing on negative information, employees may be discouraged from providing the necessary feedback to their managers.

4.9.2.   Guidelines for Effective Communication

- Senders of message must clarify in their minds what they want to communicate. Purpose of the message and making a plan to achieve the intended end must be clarified.
- Encoding and decoding be done with symbols that are familiar to the sender and the receiver of the message.
- For the planning of the communication, other people should be consulted and encouraged to participate.
- It is important to consider the needs of the receivers of the information. Whenever appropriate, one should communicate something that is of value to them, in the short run as well as in the more distant future.
- In communication, tone of voice, the choice of language and the congruency between what is said and how it is said influence the reactions of the receiver of the message,
- Communication is complete only when the message is understood by the receiver. And one never knows whether communication is understood unless the sender gets a feedback.

- The function of communication is more than transmitting the information. It also deals with emotions that are very important in interpersonal relationships between superiors, subordinates and colleagues in an organization,

- Effective communicating is the responsibility not only of the sender but also of the receiver of the information.

4.9.3. *Barriers to Effective Communication*

Barriers to communication are factors that block or significantly distort successful communication. Effective managerial communication skills helps overcome some, but not all, barriers to communication in organizations. The more prominent barriers to effective communication which every manager should be aware of is given below:

a) *Filtering*

Filtering refers to a sender manipulating information so it will be seen more favorably by the receiver. The major determinant of filtering is the number of levels in an organization's structure. The more vertical levels in the organization's hierarchy, the more opportunities for filtering. Sometimes the information is filtered by the sender himself. If the sender is hiding some meaning and disclosing in such a fashion as appealing to the receiver, then he is "filtering" the message deliberately. A manager in the process of altering communication in his favour is attempting to filter the information.

b) *Selective Perception*

Selective perception means seeing what one wants to see. The receiver, in the communication process, generally resorts to selective perception i.e., he selectively perceives the message based on the organizational requirements, the needs and characteristics, background of the employees etc. Perceptual distortion is one of the distressing barriers to the effective communication. People interpret what they see and call it a reality. In our regular activities, we tend to see those things that please us and to reject or ignore unpleasant things. Selective perception allows us to keep out dissonance (the existence of conflicting elements in our perceptual set) at a tolerable level. If we encounter something that does not fit out current image of reality, we structure the situation to minimize our dissonance. Thus, we manage to overlook many stimuli from the environment that do not fit into out current perception of the world. This process has significant implications for managerial activities. For example, the employment interviewer who expects a female job applicant to put her family ahead of her career is likely to see that in female applicants, regardless of whether the applicants feel that way or not.

c) *Emotions*

How the receiver feels at the time of receipt of information influences effectively how he interprets the information. For example, if the receiver feels that the communicator is in a jovial mood, he interprets that the information being sent by the communicator to be good and interesting. Extreme emotions and jubilation or depression are quite likely to hinder the effectiveness of communication. A person's ability to encode a message can become impaired when the person is feeling strong emotions. For example, when you are angry, it is harder to consider the other person's viewpoint and to choose words carefully. The angrier you are, the harder this task becomes. Extreme emotions - such as jubilation or depression - are most likely to hinder effective communication. In such instances, we are most prone to disregard our rational and objective thinking processes and substitute emotional judgments.

d) *Language*

Communicated message must be understandable to the receiver. Words mean different things to different people. Language reflects not only the personality of the individual but also the culture of society in which the individual is living. In organizations, people from different regions, different backgrounds, and speak different languages. People will have different academic backgrounds, different intellectual facilities, and hence the jargon they use varies. Often, communication gap arises because the language the sender is using may be incomprehensible, vague and indigestible. Language is a central element in communication. It may pose a barrier if its use obscures meaning and distorts intent. Words mean different things to different people. Age, education and cultural background are three of the more obvious variables that influence the language a person uses and the definitions he or she gives to words. Therefore, use simple, direct, declarative language.

Speak in brief sentences and use terms or words you have heard from you audience. As much as possible, speak in the language of the listener. Do not use jargon or technical language except with those who clearly understand it.

e) *Stereotyping*

Stereotyping is the application of selective perception. When we have preconceived ideas about other people and refuse to discriminate between individual behaviours, we are applying selective perception to our relationship with other people. Stereotyping is a barrier to communications because those who stereotype others use selective perception in their communication and tend to hear only those things that confirm their stereotyped images. Consequently, stereotypes become more deeply ingrained as we find more "evidence" to confirm our original opinion. Stereotyping has a convenience function in our interpersonal relations. Since people are all different, ideally we should react and interact with each person differently. To do this, however, requires considerable psychological effort. It is much easier to categorize (stereotype) people so that we can interact with them as members of a particular category. Since the number of categories is small, we end up treating many people the same even though they are quite different. Our communications, then, may be directed at an individual as a member of a category at the sacrifice of the more effective communication on a personal level.

f) Status Difference

The organizational hierarchy pose another barrier to communication within organization, especially when the communication is between employee and manager. This is so because the employee is dependent on the manager as the primary link to the organization and hence more likely to distort upward communication than either horizontal or downward communication. Effective supervisory skills make the supervisor more approachable and help reduce the risk of problems related to status differences. In addition, when employees feel secure, they are more likely to be straight forward in upward communication.

g) Use of Conflicting Signals

A sender is using conflicting signals when he or she sends inconsistent messages. A vertical message might conflict with a nonverbal one. For example, if a manager says to his employees, "If you have a problem, just come to me. My door is always open", but he looks annoyed whenever an employee knocks on his door". Then we say the manager is sending conflicting messages. When signals conflict, the receivers of the message have to decide which, if any, to believe.

h) Reluctance to Communicate

For a variety of reasons, managers are sometimes reluctant to transmit messages. The reasons could be:

- They may doubt their ability to do so.
- They may dislike or be weary of writing or talking to others.
- They may hesitate to deliver bad news because they do not want to face a negative reaction.

When someone gives in to these feelings, they become a barrier to effective communications.

i) *Projection*

Projection has two meanings.

- Projecting one's own motives into others behavior. For example, managers who are motivated by money may assume their subordinates are also motivated by it. If the subordinate's prime motive is something other than money, serious problems may arise.
- The use of defense mechanism to avoid placing blame on oneself. As a defense mechanism, the projection phenomenon operates to protect the ego from unpleasant communications. Frequently, individuals who have a particular fault will see the same fault in others, making their own fault seem not so serious.

j) *The "Halo Effect"*

The term "halo effect" refers to the process of forming opinions based on one element from a group of elements and generalizing that perception to all other elements. For example, in an organization, a good attendance record may cause positive judgments about productivity, attitude, or quality of work. In performance evaluation system, the halo effect refers to the practice of singling out one trait of an employee (either good or bad) and using this as a basis for judgments of the total employee.

4.9.4. *Channels of Communication*

a) *Formal Communication*

Formal communication follows the route formally laid down in the organization structure. There are three directions in which communications flow: downward, upward and laterally (horizontal).

i. *Downward Communication*

Downward communication involves a message travelling to one or more receivers at the lower level in the hierarchy. The message frequently involves directions or performance feedback. The downward flow of communication generally corresponds to the formal organizational communications system, which is usually synonymous with the chain of command or line of authority. This system has received a great deal of attention from both managers and behavioral scientists since it is crucial to organizational functioning.

ii.   *Upward Communication*

In upward communication, the message is directed toward a higher level in the hierarchy. It is often takes the form of progress reports or information about successes and failures of the individuals or work groups reporting to the receiver of the message. Sometimes employees also send suggestions or complaints upward through the organization's hierarchy. The upward flow of communication involves two distinct manager-subordinate activities in addition to feedback:

- The participation by employees in formal organizational decisions.
- Employee appeal is a result against formal organization decisions. The employee appeal is a result of the industrial democracy concept that provides for two-way communication in areas of disagreement.

iii.   *Horizontal Communication*

When takes place among members of the same work group, among members of work groups at the same level, among managers at the same level or among any horizontally equivalent personnel, we describe it as lateral communications. In lateral communication, the sender and receiver(s) are at the same level in the hierarchy. Formal communications that travel laterally involve employees engaged in carrying out the same or related tasks. The messages might concern advice, problem solving, or coordination of activities.

b) Informal Communication or Grapevine

Informal communication, generally associated with interpersonal communication, was primarily seen as a potential hindrance to effective organizational performance. This is no longer the case. Informal communication has become more important to ensuring the effective conduct of work in modern organizations.

Probably the most common term used for the informal communication in the workplace is "grapevine" and this communication that is sent through the organizational grapevine is often considered gossip or rumor. While grapevine communication can spread information quickly and can easily cross established organizational boundaries, the information it carries can be changed through the deletion or exaggeration crucial details thus causing the information inaccurate - even if it's based on truth.

The use of the organizational grapevine as an informal communication channel often results when employees feel threatened, vulnerable, or when the organization is experiencing change and when communication from management is restricted and not forthcoming.

4.10. Organizational Culture

Organizational culture is an idea in the field of organizational studies and management which describes the psychology, attitudes, experiences, beliefs and values (personal and cultural values) of an organization. It has been defined as "the specific collection of values and norms that are shared by people and groups in an organization and that control the way they interact with each other and with stakeholders outside the organization."

4.10.1. Elements of Organizational Culture

Johnson and Scholes described a cultural web, identifying a number of elements that can be used to describe or influence Organizational Culture in the Fig4.3.

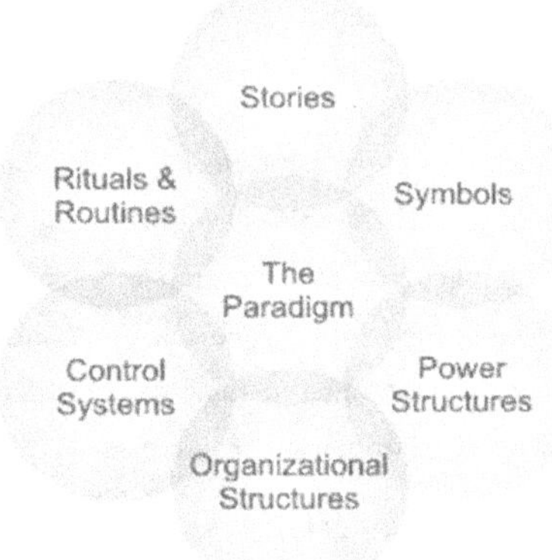

Fig 4.3: Elements of Organizational Culture

The six elements are:

a) Stories: The past events and people talked about inside and outside the company. Who and what the company chooses to immortalize says a great deal about what it values, and perceives as great behavior.

b) Rituals and Routines: The daily behavior and actions of people that signal acceptable behavior. This determines what is expected to happen in given situations, and what is valued by management.

c) Symbols: The visual representations of the company including logos, how plush the offices are, and the formal or informal dress codes.

d) Organizational Structure: This includes both the structure defined by the organization chart, and the unwritten lines of power and influence that indicate whose contributions are most valued.

e) Control Systems: The ways that the organization is controlled. These include financial systems, quality systems, and rewards (including the way they are measured and distributed within the organization.)

f) Power Structures: The pockets of real power in the company. This may involve one or two key senior executives, a whole group of executives, or even a department. The key is that these people have the greatest amount of influence on decisions, operations, and strategic direction.

4.10.2. Types of Organizational Culture

Deal and Kennedy argue organizational culture is based on based on two elements:

1. **Feedback Speed:** How quickly are feedback and rewards provided (through which the people are told they are doing a good or a bad job).

2. **Degree of Risk:** The level of risk taking (degree of uncertainty).

The combination of these two elements results in four types of corporate cultures:

a)Tough-Guy Culture or Macho Culture (Fast feedback and reward, high risk)

- Stress results from the high risk and the high potential decrease or increase of the reward.
- Focus on now, individualism prevails over teamwork.
- Typical examples: advertising, brokerage, sports.

The most important aspect of this kind of culture is big rewards and quick feedback. This kind of culture is mostly associated with quick financial activities like brokerage and currency trading. It can also be related with activities, like a sports team or branding of an athlete, and also the police team. This kind of culture is considered to carry along, a high amount of stress, and people working within the organization are expected to possess a strong mentality, for survival in the organization.

b)Work Hard/Play Hard (Fast feedback and reward, low risk)

- Stress results from quantity of work rather than uncertainty.
- Focus on high-speed action, high levels of energy.
- Typical examples: sales, restaurants, software companies.

This type of organization does not involve much risk, as the organizations already consist of a firm base along with a strong client relationship. This kind of culture is mostly opted by large organizations which have strong customer service. The organization with this kind of culture is equipped with specialized jargons and is qualified with multiple team meetings.

c)Bet Your Company Culture (Slow feedback and reward, high risk)

- Stress results from high risk and delay before knowing if actions have paid off.
- Focus on long-term, preparation and planning.
- Typical examples: pharmaceutical companies, aircraft manufacturers, oil prospecting companies.

In this kind of culture, the company makes big and important decisions over high stakes endeavors. It takes time to see the consequence of these decisions. Companies that postulate experimental projects and researches as their core business, adopt this kind of culture. This kind of culture can be adopted by a company designing experimental military weapons for example.

d)Process Culture (Slow feedback and reward, low risk)

- Stress is generally low, but may come from internal politics and stupidity of the system.
- Focus on details and process excellence.
- Typical examples: bureaucracies, banks, insurance companies, public services.

This type of culture does not include the process of feedback. In this kind of culture, the organization is extremely cautious about the adherence to laws and prefer to abide by them. This culture provides consistency to the organization and is good for public services.

One of the most difficult tasks to undertake in an organization, is to change its work culture. An organizational culture change requires an organization to make amendments to its policies, its workplace ethics and its management system. It needs to start right from its base functions which includes support functions, operations and the production floor, which finally affects the overall output of the organization. It requires a complete overhaul of the entire system, and not many organizations prefer it as the process is a long and tedious one, which requires patience and endurance. However, when an organization succeeds in making a change on such a massive level, the results are almost always positive and fruitful. The different types of organizational cultures mentioned above must have surely helped you to understand them. You can also adopt one of them for your own organization, however, persistence and patience is ultimately of the essence.

4.10.3. Managing Cultural Diversity

Experts indicate that business owners and managers who hope to create and manage an effective, harmonious multicultural work force should remember the importance of the following:

- Setting a good example-This basic tool can be particularly valuable for small business owners who hope to establish a healthy environment for people of different cultural backgrounds, since they are generally able to wield significant control over the business's basic outlook and atmosphere.

- Communicate in writing-Company policies that explicitly forbid prejudice and discriminatory behavior should be included in employee manuals, mission statements, and other written communications. Jorgensen referred to this and other similar practices as "internal broadcasting of the diversity message in order to create a common language for all members of the organization."

- Training programs-Training programs designed to engender appreciation and knowledge of the characteristics and benefits of multicultural work forces have become ubiquitous in recent years. "Two types of training are most popular: awareness and skill-building," wrote Cox. "The former introduces the topic of managing diversity and generally includes information on work force demographics, the meaning of diversity, and exercises to get participants thinking about relevant issues and raising their own self-awareness. The skill-building training provides more specific information on cultural norms of different groups and how they may affect work behavior." New employee orientation programs are also ideal for introducing workers to the company's expectations regarding treatment of fellow workers, whatever their cultural or ethnic background.

Recognize individual differences-Writing in The Complete MBA Companion, contributor Rob Goffee stated that "there are various dimensions around which differences in human relationships may be understood. These include such factors as orientation towards authority; acceptance of power inequalities; desire for orderliness and structure; the need to belong to a wider social group and so on. Around these dimensions researchers have demonstrated systematic differences between national, ethnic, and religious groups." Yet Goffee also cautioned business owners, managers, and executives to recognize that differences between individuals cannot always be traced back to easily understood differences in cultural background: "Do not assume differences are always 'cultural.' There are several sources of difference. Some relate to factors such as personality, aptitude, or competence. It is a mistake to assume that all perceived differences are cultural in origin. Too many managers tend to fall back on the easy 'explanation' that individual behavior or performance can be attributed to the fact that someone is 'Italian' or 'a Catholic' or 'a woman.' Such conclusions are more likely to reflect intellectually lazy rather than culturally sensitive managers."

- Actively seek input from minority groups-Soliciting the opinions and involvement of minority groups on important work committees, etc., is beneficial not only because of the contributions that they can make, but also because such overtures confirm that they are valued by the company. Serving on relevant committees and task forces can increase their feelings of belonging to the organization. Conversely, relegating minority members to superfluous committees or projects can trigger a downward spiral in relations between different cultural groups.

- Revamp reward systems-An organization's performance appraisal and reward systems should reinforce the importance of effective diversity management, according to Cox. This includes assuring that minorities are provided with adequate opportunities for career development.

- Make room for social events-Company sponsored social events-picnics, softball games, volleyball leagues, bowling leagues, Christmas parties, etc.-can be tremendously useful in getting members of different ethnic and cultural backgrounds together and providing them with opportunities to learn about one another.

- Don't assume similar values and opinions-Goffee noted that "in the absence of reliable information there is a well-documented tendency for individuals to assume that others are 'like them.' In any setting this is likely to be an inappropriate assumption; for those who manage diverse work forces this tendency towards 'cultural assimilation' can prove particularly damaging."

- Continuous monitoring-Experts recommend that business owners and managers establish and maintain systems that can continually monitor the organization's policies and practices to ensure that it continues to be a good environment for all employees. This, wrote Jorgensen, should include "research into employees' needs through periodic attitude surveys."

"Increased diversity presents challenges to business leaders who must maximize the opportunities that it presents while minimizing its costs," summarized Cox. "The multicultural organization is characterized by pluralism, full integration of minority-culture members both formally and informally, an absence of prejudice and discrimination, and low levels of inter-group conflict. The organization that achieves these conditions will create an environment in which all members can contribute to their maximum potential, and in which the 'value in diversity' can be fully realized."

UNIT V

CONTROLLING

Definition

Control is the process through which managers assure that actual activities conform to planned activities.

In the words of Koontz and O'Donnell - "Managerial control implies measurement of accomplishment against the standard and the correction of deviations to assure attainment of objectives according to plans."

5.1.   Nature & Purpose of Control

- Control is an essential function of management
- Control is an ongoing process
- Control is forward -working because pas cannot be controlled
- Control involves measurement
- The essence of control is action
- Control is an integrated system

5.2.   Control Process

The basic control process involves mainly these steps as shown in Fig 5.1.

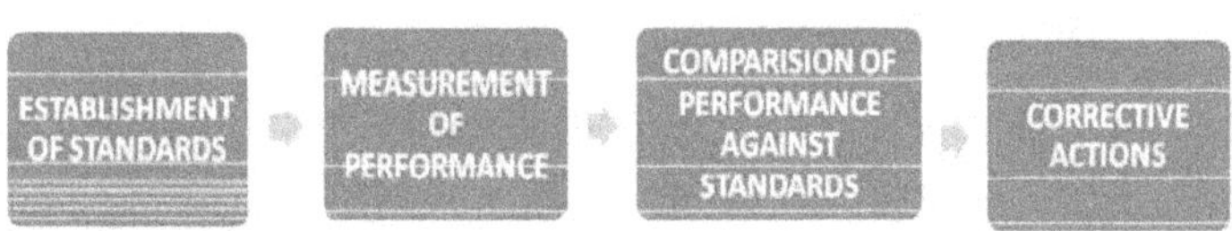

Fig 5.1: Control Process

a) The Establishment of Standards

Because plans are the yardsticks against which controls must be revised, it follows logically that the first step in the control process would be to accomplish plans. Plans can be considered as the criterion or the standards against which we compare the actual performance in order to figure out the deviations.

Examples for the standards

- Profitability standards: In general, these standards indicate how much the company would like to make as profit over a given time period- that is, its return on investment.

- Market position standards: These standards indicate the share of total sales in a particular market that the company would like to have relative to its competitors.

- Productivity standards: How much that various segments of the organization should produce is the focus of these standards.

- Product leadership standards: These indicate what must be done to attain such a position.

- Employee attitude standards: These standards indicate what types of attitudes the company managers should strive to indicate in the company's employees.

- Social responsibility standards: Such as making contribution to the society.

- Standards reflecting the relative balance between short and long range goals.

b) Measurement of Performance

The measurement of performance against standards should be on a forward looking basis so that deviations may be detected in advance by appropriate actions. The degree of difficulty in measuring various types of organizational performance, of course, is determined primarily by the activity being measured. For example, it is far more difficult to measure the performance of highway maintenance worker than to measure the performance of a student enrolled in a college level management course.

c) Comparing Measured Performance to Stated Standards

When managers have taken a measure of organizational performance, their next step in controlling is to compare this measure against some standard. A standard is the level of activity established to serve as a model for evaluating organizational performance. The performance evaluated can be for the organization as a whole or for some individuals working within the organization. In essence, standards are the yardsticks that determine whether organizational performance is adequate or inadequate.

d) Taking Corrective Actions

After actual performance has been measured compared with established performance standards, the next step in the controlling process is to take corrective action, if necessary. Corrective action is managerial activity aimed at bringing organizational performance up to the level of performance standards. In other words, corrective action focuses on correcting organizational mistakes that hinder organizational performance. Before taking any corrective action, however, managers should make sure that the standards they are using were properly established and that their measurements of organizational performance are valid and reliable. At first glance, it seems a fairly simple proposition that managers should take corrective action to eliminate problems - the factors within an organization that are barriers to organizational goal attainment. In practice, however, it is often difficult to pinpoint the problem causing some undesirable organizational effect.

5.3.   Barriers for Controlling

There are many barriers, among the most important of them:

- Control activities can create an undesirable overemphasis on short-term production as opposed to long- term production.
- Control activities can increase employees' frustration with their jobs and thereby reduce morale. This reaction tends to occur primarily where management exerts too much control.
- Control activities can encourage the falsification of reports.
- Control activities can cause the perspectives of organization members to be too narrow for the good of the organization.
- Control activities can be perceived as the goals of the control process rather than the means by which corrective action is taken.

5.4.   Requirements for Effective Control

The requirements for effective control are

- Control should be tailored to plans and positions: This means that, all control techniques and systems should reflect the plans they are designed to follow. This is because every plan and every kind and phase of an operation has its unique characteristics.
- Control must be tailored to individual managers and their responsibilities: This means that controls must be tailored to the personality of individual managers. This because control systems and information are intended to help individual managers carry out their function of control. If they are not of a type that a manager can or will understand, they will not be useful.

- Control should point up exceptions as critical points: This is because by concentration on exceptions from planned performance, controls based on the time honored exception principle allow managers to detect those places where their attention is required and should be given. However, it is not enough to look at exceptions, because some deviations from standards have little meaning and others have a great deal of significance.

- Control should be objective: This is because when controls are subjective, a manager's personality may influence judgments of performance inaccuracy. Objective standards can be quantitative such as costs or man hours per unit or date of job completion. They can also be qualitative in the case of training programs that have specific characteristics or are designed to accomplish a specific kind of upgrading of the quality of personnel.

- Control should be flexible: This means that controls should remain workable in the case of changed plans, unforeseen circumstances, or outsight failures. Much flexibility in control can be provided by having alternative plans for various probable situations.

- Control should be economical: This means that control must worth their cost. Although this requirement is simple, its practice is often complex. This is because a manager may find it difficult to know what a particular system is worth, or to know what it costs.

- Control should lead to corrective actions: This is because a control system will be of little benefit if it does not lead to corrective action, control is justified only if the indicated or experienced deviations from plans are corrected through appropriate planning, organizing, directing, and leading.

5.5.   Types of Control Systems

The control systems can be classified into three types namely feed forward, concurrent and feedback control systems. The various types of control system is explained in the following Fig 5.2

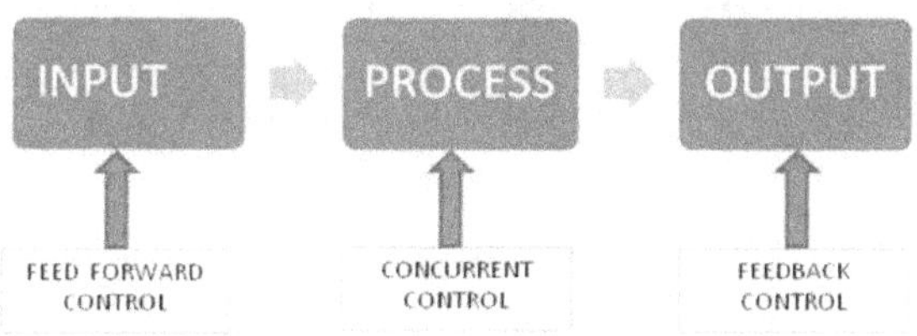

Fig 5.2: Control Systems

a) **Feed forward controls:** They are preventive controls that try to anticipate problems and take corrective action before they occur. Example-a team leader checks the quality, completeness and reliability of their tools prior to going to the site.

b) **Concurrent controls:** They (sometimes called screening controls) occur while an activity is taking place. Example - the team leader checks the quality or performance of his members while performing.

c) **Feedback controls:** They measure activities that have already been completed. Thus corrections can take place after performance is over. Example - feedback from facilities engineers regarding the completed job.

5.6. Budgetary Control

Definition: Budgetary Control is defined as "the establishment of budgets, relating the responsibilities of executives to the requirements of a policy, and the continuous comparison of actual with budgeted results either to secure by individual action the objective of that policy or to provide a base for its revision.

Salient Features

a) **Objectives:** Determining the objectives to be achieved, over the budget period, and the policy(ies) that might be adopted for the achievement of these ends.

b) **Activities:** Determining the variety of activities that should be undertaken for achievement of the objectives.

c) **Plans:** Drawing up a plan or a scheme of operation in respect of each class of activity, in physical as well as monetary terms for the full budget period and its parts.

d) **Performance Evaluation:** Laying out a system of comparison of actual performance by each person section or department with the relevant budget and determination of causes for the discrepancies, if any.

e) **Control Action:** Ensuring that when the plans are not achieved, corrective actions are taken; and when corrective actions are not possible, ensuring that the plans are revised and objective achieved

5.6.1. Classification of Budgets

Budgets may be classified on the following Fig 5.3.

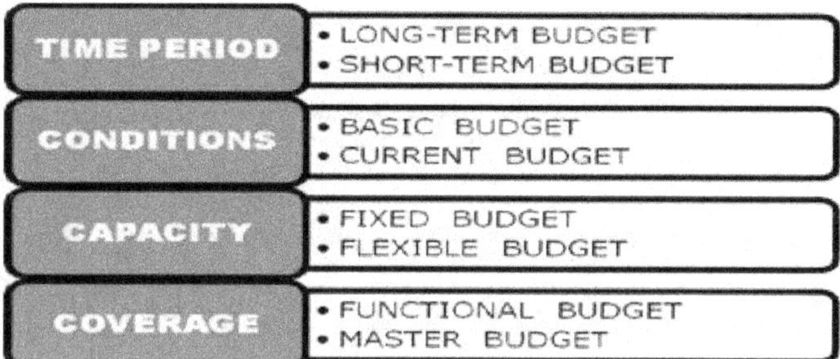

Fig 5.3: Classification of Budgets

a) Based on Time Period

i. Long Term Budget

Budgets which are prepared for periods longer than a year are called Long Term Budgets. Such Budgets are helpful in business forecasting and forward planning. Eg: Capital Expenditure Budget and R&D Budget,

ii. Short Term Budget

Budgets which are prepared for periods less than a year are known as Short Term Budgets. Such Budgets are prepared in cases where a specific action has to be immediately taken to bring any variation under control. Eg: Cash Budget.

b) Based on Condition

i. Basic Budget

A Budget, which remains unaltered over a long period of time, is called Basic Budget,

ii. Current Budget

A Budget, which is established for use over a short period of time and is related to the current conditions, is called Current Budget.

c) Based on Capacity

i. Fixed Budget

It is a Budget designed to remain unchanged irrespective of the level of activity actually attained. It operates on one level of activity and less than one set of conditions. It assumes that there will be no change in the prevailing conditions, which is unrealistic,

ii. Flexible Budget

It is a Budget, which by recognizing the difference between fixed, semi variable and variable costs is designed to change in relation to level of activity attained. It consists of various budgets for different levels of activity.

d) Based on Coverage

i. Functional Budget

Budgets, which relate to the individual functions in an organization, are known as Functional Budgets, e.g. purchase Budget, Sales Budget, Production Budget, plant Utilization Budget and Cash Budget,

ii. Master Budget

It is a consolidated summary of the various functional budgets. It serves as the basis upon which budgeted Profit & Loss Account and forecasted Balance Sheet are built up.

5.6.2. Budget ARY Control Techniques

The various types of budgets are as follows

i. Revenue and Expense Budgets

The most common budgets spell out plans for revenues and operating expenses in rupee terms. The most basic of revenue budget is the sales budget which is a formal and detailed expression of the sales forecast. The revenue from sales of products or services furnishes the principal income to pay operating expenses and yield profits. Expense budgets may deal with individual items of expense, such as travel, data processing, entertainment, advertising, telephone, and insurance.

ii. Time, Space, Material, and Product Budgets

Many budgets are better expressed in quantities rather than in monetary terms, e.g. direct-labor-hours, machine-hours, units of materials, square feet allocated, and units produced. The Rupee cost would not accurately measure the resources used or the results intended.